THE FATHERLY RULE OF GOD

THE FATHERLY RULE OF GOD

OF GOD

A Study of Society, State and Church

By

REV. ALFRED E. GARVIE

M.A.(Oxon.), D.D.(Glasgow and London), D.Th.(Berlin.)

" Render unto Cæsar the things that are Cæsar's ;
and unto God the things that are God's."

LONDON
HODDER AND STOUGHTON LIMITED
PUBLISHERS

First printed in 1935

PRINTED AND BOUND IN GREAT BRITAIN FOR HODDER AND STOUGHTON, LIMITED
BY RICHARD CLAY AND SONS, LIMITED, BUNGAY, SUFFOLK.

DEDICATED TO

THE MEMBERS, PAST AND PRESENT, OF THE
UNIVERSAL CHRISTIAN COUNCIL FOR LIFE AND
WORK, WITH WHOM IT HAS BEEN MY PRIVILEGE
IN FORMER YEARS TO HOLD CHRISTIAN
FELLOWSHIP, TO TAKE COUNSEL AND CO-OPERATE
IN THE SERVICE OF THE KINGDOM OF GOD,
"OUR FATHER IN HEAVEN."

PREFACE

THE perilous condition of Continental Protestantism in relation to the Governments has led the *Universal Christian Council for Life and Work*, the continuation of the Stockholm Conference of 1925, to decide that the special subject for study and consideration at the next Conference in 1937 shall be *Church, Community, and State*; and small conferences and group and individual studies are being pursued in different countries in preparation for that Conference. A small conference was held in Paris in April 1934, and a second edition of the German Report of that Conference has recently appeared under the title, *Die Kirche und das Staatsproblem in der Gegenwart;* an English and a French edition are in preparation. Vigorous action to further the object is being taken in Great Britain by a Commission under the Chairmanship of Dr. Oldham of the International Missionary Council, who has just published a pamphlet under the title, *Church, Community, and State*, in which he indicates the importance and the urgency of the problem. This has been the immediate occasion for this book; but the motives to, and the reasons for the writing of it go much further back. The Stockholm Conference of 1925, following the " Copec " Conference in Birmingham in 1924 on the one hand, and the Lausanne Conference on Faith and Order of 1927 on the other, gave a more definite direction to practical interests and theoretical studies of many previous years; and the occasion confirmed the desire to deal with the subjects of this volume.

While I may have some share in these preparations for the Conference, I do not cherish the hope of being present in 1937, as a man over seventy is wise in realising that he has pitched his moving tent on " borrowed ground," and cannot confidently reckon on health and strength, even if life is spared, to work as he has hitherto had the joy of doing; and for that reason I feel justified in now giving expression to my convictions on this theme.

Further, the subject of the relation of Church and State, especially in Germany, is one of so urgent importance and acute interest, that anyone who, like myself, has had exceptional facilities for keeping himself informed on the course of events is under obligation to share his knowledge with others so that they may be guided to a right judgment. Again, I hope that this book may have some value, however slight, as a contribution to the discussions of the next two years. It makes no pretensions to be an adequate historical study, such as it is hoped to stimulate, nor to expound the views of any particular confessions such as are found in the Report of the Paris Conference, and are likely to be offered by others. The standpoint is distinctively individual, and in it I have fused together, as the teaching of Jesus justifies, the complementary conceptions of God's Fatherhood and of the Kingdom of God in the one idea of what my loved and honoured teacher, Dr. Fairbairn, called the *paternal sovereignty*, but which I have in the title described as the *Fatherly Rule of God*. It is this idea, not any of natural law, creative order, which I have tried to make the regulative principle of the whole discussion. This individual approach to the subject may, I hope, be not without value for the general discussion, which will engage many minds in many lands. I have drawn up a list of a few publications which I have found useful, and which may be useful to others, but which makes no claim to be an adequate bibliography. I have reviewed most of them within the last two years in *The Expository Times*; several articles on the German situation in *The Christian World* have brought me so many generous expressions of appreciation, and I have been so often asked to give addresses or lectures upon it within this last year, that I hope, to use the current economic phrases, this supply will meet with an effective demand and not be condemned as over-production. In the discussions I have sufficiently stressed the gravity of the situation, the magnitude of the issues involved, and the necessity that the best minds in the churches be applied to the study. It is therefore not inappropriate that I should close with the prayer that should become general: "May the Spirit of Truth guide the Church as the Witness of that Truth into the Truth, so that the Kingdoms of this world shall become the Kingdoms of our God and of His Christ."

ALFRED E. GARVIE.

London,
  March, 1935.

CONTENTS

B

A S the subject of this volume is the relation of the State and the Church, the treatment must be theological, since the problem can find its solution only as the purpose of God for man in society through the two most prominent associations—State and Church—is made the guiding principle.

(1) What God's purpose for man is must be determined by the conception we form of the relation of God and Man. The *ethical monotheism* of the Hebrew prophets, as completed in the revelation of God as Father in Jesus as Christ and Lord and through the Holy Spirit, is here assumed as consistent with, though not discovered by, human reason, as realised in human history, and as confirmed in human experience; but it may be briefly summarised.

(*a*) The metaphysical attributes of God accepted as intelligible and credible are His infinitude, as transcendence of all limitations other than those due to His nature, character, and purpose as God, His absoluteness, as transcendence of any dependence on any other reality, His immensity and

His eternity as transcendence of the conditions of the finite, dependent world—space and time, His immanence in the world as omnipresent, omniscient and omnipotent. With these attributes the conception of personality, not in its human actuality, but as the human mind can conceive it as ideal, as self-limiting and self-depending perfection, can be shown to be consistent; while it may be admitted that beyond and above God's personal relation to man there may be ranges and reaches of His reality which man's most ideal conception of personality cannot measure, in His totality God may be described as *supra-personal*, just as in His relation to man He may be apprehended as *personal*.

(*b*) The human ideals—truth, beauty, goodness—have their eternal reality in His personal perfection. The attributes of that personal perfection may be stated to be truth and wisdom (corresponding to human reason and conscience), holiness the perfection which distinguishes God from man's imperfection, righteousness in asserting and maintaining His holiness in His relations to man in his sinfulness, goodness in bestowing His gifts of care and bounty upon man, love in making man in His likeness and for fellowship with Himself, grace in the exercise of that love in relation to man as sinful—in propitiation, redemption, reconciliation. While God's intellec-

tual and volitional attributes have been readily
recognised by philosophers and theologians, there
has been hesitancy about assigning any emotional;
but for the religious consciousness the personal
relation to God would lack much if God were
subject to the limitation of a passionless mono-
tony of blessedness; if He could not feel with and
for man—joy or sorrow. Hence in God's relation
to the world we may dare to add the attribute of
omnipatience. Here may be added a qualification
of what has been stated above regarding God's
transcendence of the conditions of space and time
—namely, that if God is personally immanent in
His world, time and space must have as much
reality for Him as the world of which these are the
conditions; otherwise it would seem as if human
history on earth could have no meaning or worth
for Him. This impossibility would strike at the
very root of the Hebrew and Christian conception
of God, who has in time and space revealed Himself to man to save and bless.

(*c*) This revelation of God to the Hebrew nation
was by the succession of inspired prophets, men
conscious of having been called to their mission,
and equipped with their message by God Himself
through His enlightening, quickening and renewing Spirit within man. This revelation is completed by the Incarnation of the Son of God, God
as Son more immediately present in, and intimately

related to, human personality in Jesus than in any inspired prophet, so that God as man and in man made Himself known to men for redemption and reconciliation. Consequent on the Incarnation and the human communion with God thereby mediated, the presence and activity of God through His Spirit was experienced in the community of believers in Christ, who accepted Him as Saviour and Lord. Thus the ethical monotheism was expanded into the conception of the one God as Father, Son, and Holy Spirit as men experienced the love of God as Father through the grace of the Lord Jesus Christ in the communion of the Holy Spirit (II Cor. xiii. 14). The Christian doctrine of the Trinity is the necessary theological interpretation of this experience.

(2) In describing God as personal and in personal relations with man in His love and grace in Christ and in His activity as Spirit in man, as the reality of the human ideals in perfection, the conception of man corresponding to this conception of God has been already indicated.

(a) As personal man thinks, feels, wills; he possesses liberty and responsibility to realise in his character and conduct the ideals of truth, beauty and goodness: he can wrest her secrets from Nature, control her forces and command her resources in a progressive advance in culture and civilisation; he can enter into personal relations with his fellow-men as he develops socially in forming associations and institutions; but, what for our present purpose is most significant: he is aware of God, the reality *above and beyond* his world and himself, and yet *akin to and within* himself. His religion gives a fuller meaning and a higher worth to his civilisation and culture, the realisation of his ideals, his social relations to others, for in his knowledge of God he reaches the ultimate cause and the final purpose of all things, the infinite significance of the finite, the eternal value of the temporal. As in God's light he looks on world and self, he comes to know the world as God wills that its meaning should be understood, and that his own worth should be realised.

(*b*) This, it may be said, is the ideal; how unlike is the actual! For has not sin marred the likeness to God, and disturbed the fellowship with God? Has not man in his history proved himself a tragic mistake and failure? To minimise the consequences of man's sin is a fatal falsehood; for it is only the self-discovery of man as sinner that can be the beginning of self-recovery as son of God and as saint. We must not exaggerate man's undoing by his sin; it has not gone so far as to destroy beyond recovery his promise and his potency as God has made him. The lost is not beyond the reach of God's finding and saving grace (Luke xix. 10)—the restoration by the creative, renewing Spirit of God of the ruin to become the temple of God. Not only is the incarnate Son the recapitulation of mankind according to God's creative intention as pattern, but also as power. Creation is restored in redemption and reconciliation; and we can cherish " the larger hope " that the God who has the resources to create has also the resources fully to redeem and reconcile so that where sin abounded grace shall more exceedingly abound (Romans v. 20).

(3) Owing to some recent tendencies to reaction which would once more identify the Gospel of Jesus Christ with doctrines necessarily superseded in the light of modern knowledge and thought, it seems necessary to examine more closely the three conceptions of Creation, Providence and Revelation.

(a) Ever and again there appear in the newspapers declarations of men of science, which are acclaimed by a few theologians, that the theory of evolution has been discredited and that Darwin has been proved a deceiver. Even were this true, it would be irrelevant to the defence of the Gospel; and they are misguided defenders of the Christian faith who would make its validity dependent on the adequacy or inadequacy of any scientific theory. Not the divine content of the Gospel is affected by changes of human thought, but only the theological formulation. The recognised inadequacy of the Darwinian theory has not led men of science generally to abandon the conception of Evolution as the most efficiently working hypothesis in the investigation of nature. Accordingly, we may still most intelligibly think of evolution as the divine method of Creation, a progressive process as the expression of an unfolding purpose of God. The descriptions in Genesis i. and ii. of the process may yield to the wonderful story science unfolds, but the religious truth that God is Creator remains. Even if an unbroken continuity of matter, life, and mind, plant, animal and man, were demonstrated, as the phrases current in science and philosophy, *creative* and *emergent*, show has not been done, that truth would remain unshaken, because God must not be thought as being outside the process as a whole, and coming into it only at the gaps in the continuity which still exist for science. All a Christian theism needs to insist on is that the higher stages in the evolution are not resolvable into the lower, man to animal, mind to matter; even if " the missing links " were discovered, the difference would need to be recognised. Although men have speculated about the existence of life in other parts of the Universe, there is no convincing evidence of the fact, and our theology need not now concern itself with such speculations. As far as our knowledge reaches, man is the highest product of this process; he is the world come to "self-knowledge, self-reverence, self-control." He can look outward on his environment, backward on his history, inward on his own nature, upward to his own ideals and the reality of God, and he can translate ideas and ideals into fact; within his capacity and opportunity he shares the creative process. His animal ancestry survives, and limits, but his distinctive human equipment can and does transform his inheritance.

(*b*) For that reason it is not an adequate account of man's sinfulness that it is due entirely to a survival of the animal appetites and impulses, which the human endowment of reason and conscience and will come in too late in his development to control from the beginning, so that the moral race starts in every case with a handicap. A human babe is never merely an animal, whatever the appearances may be; but from the beginning the human endowment is modifying the animal inheritance, and the human environment is affecting the development of this human endowment. The social inheritance through nurture must be recognised as a potent factor in this development as well as the physical heredity of nature. Racial evolution and individual development seem to me to be adequate to explain, so far as explanation is possible, human sinfulness without the assumption of a fall of the first ancestors. Unless we accept Genesis iii. as authentic history, we are not justified in describing mankind as only a fallen race. Mankind has fallen and is falling into sin, but has also risen and is rising into goodness. Man's history has been a chequered career, but not unmitigated tragedy, still less continuous triumph. I hold as clearly and firmly as any advocate of Augustinianism or Calvinism could hold man's sinfulness, his inability to save himself, his need and the sufficiency of the grace of God in Christ; but in view of all the facts such phrases as natural corruption, total depravity, original sin have for me become anachronisms. Pelagianism and Arminianism are just as inadequate, as in opposing human liberty to divine sovereignty they are no less entangled in a false antithesis, and throw the emphasis on man's freedom as contrasted with God's grace. The relation between God and man is so immediate, that man realises himself personally as he lives with, in, and for God. I have laid such stress on these considerations, as on the doctrine of man's fall there is based a view of the State which appears to me absolutely false—namely, that God has appointed the State as a restraint on sin by the exercise of force, so that force is of its essence. That view will be opposed in a subsequent chapter, but meanwhile what needs to be affirmed is that, serious as are the consequences of human sin, not for man only, but for God also, if He shares, as has been maintained, in the life of man, we are indulging in baseless speculations when we attempt to distinguish the purpose of God before and after sin had appeared in mankind.

(*c*) While it is convenient to distinguish phases of the divine activity, such as Creation, Providence, Revelation and Redemption—yet identity of purpose and continuity of action must always be recognised, so that distinction should not be allowed to lapse into separation. So far as man can read the record of the heavens, stars are in the making and unmaking, and the man of science is not quite so confident about the indestructibility of matter, the transformation of energy, the running down of the Universe, as he once was. Creation may be going on at this moment even in the physical Universe. Is there not a mental, moral and spiritual creation going on in mankind? Old things are passing away and all things are becoming new (II Cor. v. 17). Do we assign to Jesus Christ our Lord His full cosmic as well as human significance, unless in His Resurrection, or even the Incarnation itself we recognise a fresh stage in the process of Creation, the suprahuman stage of a divine–human order of the sons of God? (Romans viii. 19).   It is a false dualism so to separate the physical Universe from the human evolution as to confine the divine creative activity to the one, and exclude it from the other. God is ever Creator.

(4) We may make a relative distinction between *Creation* and *Conservation* as an element in Divine Providence in some such way as this:

(*a*) *Creation* is the bringing into existence within the finite, temporal sphere of something new out of the infinite and eternal resources of God, *Conservation* is the maintenance of what exists in existence, and that no less depends on God's continuous activity.   The world does not exist of itself, or by itself, although God gives it in the self-limitation of His activity a relative permanence and independence; but ultimately God maintains its existence.   Physical forces are a finite exercise of infinite Power, and natural laws a finite expression of infinite Wisdom.   This conservation of what already exists is the condition of the Creation of all that comes to be.   Physical conditions and chemical processes are necessary to life, and are preserved though transformed in the organism; and so the vital organism is the organ of mental activity; in man animal appetites can be sublimated into personal affections.   There is progress with continuity.

(*b*) God's *Providence* is such a direction and

control of created and conserved reality as serves
the ends of the Divine Purpose for mankind.
There is nothing arbitrary or artificial about God's
activity here.   How puerile has the representation of God's Providence been, not only in popular
piety, but even in man's non-rational theology!
There are three errors which need to be corrected.
First of all God's Providence is according to His
purpose for the good of mankind; it is not at the
command of individual or corporate desires and
plans which are not consistent with it.   Days of
intercession could not prevail to enlist God in the
ranks of Great Britain or Germany in the Great
War.   God's care and bounty embrace all his
human children and take account of each as well
as all (Matt. vi. 25–34).   This universal bene-
ficence is distributed in individual benefits; but
there is no partiality in His goodness and grace;
heaven has neither its victims nor its favourites.
In our individual relation to Him—for He loves
each man as well as all mankind—we may with a
childlike thankfulness praise Him for the good
which comes to us, and with a childlike trustful-
ness make our wants and wishes known; but we
may not ask Him to take sides with us against
others, or expect favours which might leave others
unblessed.   The more we individually place God's
purpose above every ambition or even aspiration
of our own, the greater can be our confidence that

all things will work for our good according to His holy and blessed will (Rom. viii. 28).

Secondly, it is not a recognition of Divine Providence to acquiesce in all events as God's will. In man's history stupidity and folly, greed and pride, wickedness and cruelty have been so general and so potent factors, that, as the petition in the Lord's Prayer indicates, we must confess that God's Kingdom has not yet come in its adequate and final triumph, because His will is not being done on earth as it is done in heaven (Matt. vi. 10). God does so guide the course of events to guard against mankind's going altogether astray, and to bring man's doings under His ordering; but that guidance is no occasional and arbitrary intervention. If man's choices are not externally determined, the consequences of His actions are determined by the inexorable law that " as a man soweth so shall he reap "; if he sow to the flesh, he will reap corruption, and if he sow to the Spirit, he will reap eternal life (Gal. vi. 7, 8). God's purpose is a steadfast and not a wayward purpose; and there is an inevitable sequence in the moral as in the natural order. God's judgment is no infliction of penalty unrelated to the offence, nor His mercy a prevention of the consequences which the pardoned sin involves for self and others, unless in so far as the changed life brings a counteractive agency into play. It is not piety but presumption to act according to the dictates of our conscience without considering what it may involve, leaving the consequences to God, and expecting Him by miracle to correct our mistakes.

Thirdly, God respects the natural and the moral order which express His constancy of wisdom and goodness, and the identifying of God's providence with unusual occurrences as interferences with either order is not religion but superstition. The vastness and the mystery of the Universe, the uniformity of nature, the same physical forces and the same natural laws displayed in the making of an atom as in the making of a star, the same recompense or retribution following individual choices, or general policies—these, and not unusual occurrences, are the more convincing evidences of the infinite power and eternal wisdom of God's Providence, His directing and controlling activity in His world. What confusion there would be in man's knowledge of the world, what chaos in his doing in the world, if he could not absolutely rely on God's constancy !

Lastly, as God's activity is not an inflexible mechanical, but an adaptable personal, the fulfilment of His purpose takes account of what in man's doings helps or hinders. If man's sinfulness and all its consequences involve such a delay of, and obstacle to, that fulfilment as the world's

history which is also its judgment allows us to
assume, then it is not inconsistent with what has
just been argued to admit that what seem to us
men, with our limited understanding, abnormal
means may be needed to restore normality
according to God's will. God's revelation of Himself and His redemption of man may transcend
the natural and the moral order as disclosed in
common experience, transcend, not disturb or
destroy. Just as life transcends physical conditions and chemical processes in the organism without annulling them, or mind the organism, so
grace may transcend nature as we know it, and
God may fulfil Himself in *wonders*, *powers and
signs* without inconstancy.   Nay, rather in fidelity
to the highest end of all His works and ways.   As
has already been indicated, the Incarnation is a
new stage in God's Creation, and thus may disclose forces and laws that the lower stages could
not yet convey. We may on sufficient evidence
admit miracle as fact, but we must not interpret
it as divine interference with physical forces or
violation of natural laws. The supernatural, if
with our restricted view of nature we must call it
so, is no contradiction, but the completion of the
natural, for it is the same God, who creates and
redeems.

(5) Gnosticism distinguished the Creator from
the Redeemer God, but the Church truly and

c

rightly—the great Father Irenæus notably—
rejected that separation, and preserved monotheism, the belief in God as one and alone.

(a) A more subtle and even less reasonable
dualism affirms the one God, but contrasts what
He is as Creator and as Redeemer. The Old
Testament recognises a revelation of God in the
natural as in the moral order, as in Psalm xix.
Jesus saw the presence and activity of His
heavenly Father in His care for the birds of the
air and the flowers of the field (Matt. vi. 25–34).
For Him Nature was not " red in tooth and claw."
The imagery He uses from the ways of Nature and
the works of men shows that He did not feel Himself to be in an alien world, but even here at home
with God. He recognises man's sinfulness—His
sickness, his debt, His lostness, and He sought by
service and sacrifice to save, but sin had not exiled
God from His world, or destroyed in men the
capacity to become the children of God. He
made His appeal to man's reason and conscience,
still capable of receiving truth and responding to
grace. Paul paints mankind in darker hues
(Rom. i. ii.), and doubtless the pagan world
betrayed a corruption and superstition that were
not so familiar to Jesus; and yet He recognises a
revelation of God in Nature and in conscience.
Is it intelligible or is it credible that God should
hide Himself from honest believers and sincere

worshippers? God has been found whenever and wherever He has been sought; nay, man seeks because God is seeking him. Wherever and whenever there has been human sight there has been divine light—nay, the physical analogy suggests that it is the light which evokes the sight when there is the needed sensitiveness.

(b) There is a revelation of God in Nature and man; and this does not depreciate the value of the unique, incomparable revelation to the Hebrew prophets, and in the Incarnate Son. To banish God afar from all mankind is not to assure ourselves that He is near in one people or one person. The gradual development of the knowledge of God in the Hebrew people, the human conditions of the consciousness of His sonship and God's Fatherhood in Jesus Himself, the characteristics of the Pauline and Johannine witness to the Word of God—all forbid our putting an abysmal gulf between this revelation and all the other media through which God has willed to make Himself known. This fuller and clearer revelation has doubtless made it possible for us to discern God more surely in His world than we otherwise could have done: but rejoicing in the noontide splendour, let our more sensitive sight more gladly discern wherever we can the gleams of dawn. Creation and Providence are also Revelation, if less than Redemption is.

(*c*) It may be asked, How is it, if God wills thus to reveal Himself, that the revelation in Nature and history has proved so imperfect and inadequate? There must be sight as well as light; there must be in man a capacity to receive and respond to the communication of God. God's creative method in the race has been evolution, in the individual development; there is a correspondence between the *macrocosm* and the *microcosm*. This gradualness seems a necessity of created existence, cosmic, animal or human, and we may be sure that that necessity is not imposed on God, but expresses His wisdom and goodness. By this gradualness God gives a share to His creatures in the creative process; each stage is a condition of the next. Infinite power condescends to be exercised with and through finite forces. Still more does the organism contribute to its own growth, and the dignity and dower of personality is self-development. If a human analogy may be used, does not the parent rejoice in the growth of his child, guiding and guarding the self-development? Would any mother wish her child to come to her other than as the helpless babe, and is his prattle not music in her ears? Does not the artist or the author delight in his picture or book as it advances step to step under his hand? If the motive of Creation be love, does not God delight in His own creating? We may affirm that the method of Revelation corresponds to the method of Creation, for God is " without variation or shadow of turning " (Jas. i. 17). All doctrines of revelation which represent it as " a bolt from the blue," as omnipotence reducing man to impotence, as a communication which does not evoke a receptivity and responsiveness the capacity for which is latent in man, and thus made patent, are false in theory and contrary to the facts as the record of revelation presents the process. It is the same glory of the only-begotten of the Father, but how differently is it mirrored in the Johannine and the Pauline literature! Hence the inadequacy and imperfection are not in God's imparting, but in man's conveying what is thus given. Man is the organ of God's activity not as a passive puppet, but as an active person. Incalculable as have been the consequences of man's sin in perverting reason and obscuring conscience, sin has not so far prevailed against God in " His masterpiece man " as to make man incapable of recovery of his innate capacity for God, when faith responds to the grace which evokes it.

(6) Thus are we led to recognise that because man is sinful, the revelation of God must be redemption.

(a) Men have speculated as to what the world would have been without sin. If we dare not speak with Augustine of *beata culpa*—sin the occasion of God's grace—we cannot conceive a revelation not redemptive as more excellently revealing God than one that is redemptive. We may hold with Calvin that Incarnation as the only adequate and perfect medium of revelation would have crowned a sinless race, and yet Christ without His Cross would not shed a greater radiance. We must beware of too intellectualist a view of redemption. A theory of atonement or a plan of salvation to be believed may lessen the significance and lower the value of the fact of Christ and His Cross. This sacrifice for salvation is a *fact*, a deed done by God in Christ once for all (Rom. vi. 10), identifying God as self-giving love with the human history. Hence the inadequacy of any representation of Christ only as Teacher, Example, Leader, or any comparison of Him as such with Confucius, Gautama, Zoroaster, Mohammed. There is a deed of God in Christ, solitary and final, but universal and permanent in its effects.

(*b*) To give this centrality to Christ and His Cross—and that includes the Incarnation as its condition, and the Resurrection as its complement—is to invest human history with the significance and the value of divine revelation in human redemption. It is not a fortuitous succession of ages, even if marked by progress for man and evolution for nature, but it has a necessary plan as the fulfilment of the divine purpose. In the fulfilment of that purpose God *acts* (action including passion, achievement, endurance) first of all in man as object of His saving sovereignty and then through man as organ of it. That man as conscious free personality may become God's partner in that purpose he must be changed from rebel to son, from sinner to saint. Although God, who is unchanging, was redeeming men from sin and reconciling them unto Himself before Calvary; and we must recognise the evidences of grace in the Old Testament and elsewhere (Psalm li., Isaiah liii.), yet the light of divine truth and the warmth of divine love, often feebly diffused in history, are here focused so as to reveal the mystery of the ages. And since the Cross the Risen Saviour and Lord has been radiating that same light and heat throughout the world.

(*c*) God's Creation is His Revelation of Himself, and His Revelation is Redemption of mankind. The attempt to assign this or that activity of God to Creation, or to Providence in distinction from His action in Christ is mistaken and misleads. " The solemn shadow of that Cross is better than the sun," and in that light only can we see light clearly on nature and history. Not only the Church, but the State also must be related to the redemptive order. There and there only can be found the clue to guide us through the labyrinth. To distinguish between the natural, the social and the charismatic order, as an absolute distinction, so as to exclude the evangelical principles from the other spheres is arbitrarily to divide God's one world, which has its unity made manifest in the redemptive purposes in Christ and His Cross. If this conclusion be true, as I believe it is true, a great deal of ancient theological lumber can be disregarded. Our duty is not to galvanise dead theologies into apparent life but to seek a living theology, which the ever-present and active Spirit of God, the Life-Giver, will impart to us as we seek His gifts.

(7) As we shall be concerned in the following chapters with human personality as social, whatever be the form or the object of society with which we shall be immediately dealing, it is important for our purpose to base our conception of society not on human expedient or artifice, but on God's purpose as that expresses God's nature. While we must guard our monotheism against the danger of tritheism, yet the doctrine of the Trinity, or Tri-unity, God as Father, Son, and Holy Spirit is the distinctive Christian conception. God is not a bare unit, but difference-in-unity. We cannot conceive Him as personal, still less as perfectly personal, unless we recognise that He

is social personality. If Love be His eternal
reality, there must be in the very nature of God
distinctions, corresponding to, even if transcendent of the differences in this revelation of
Himself. If, as I shall try to show in dealing with
the Church, the love of God in the grace of Christ
can be personally experienced only as " the
common possession "—" the community " of the
Holy Spirit " (II Cor. xiii. 14), then not the
isolated individual, but human society, ultimately
corporate humanity, expresses God as difference-
in-unity in His revelation of Himself in history.
If I may be as bold as to apply the language of the
creeds to theories of society, *individualism* divides
the substance, as *collectivism* confuses the persons
of humanity as God's organ for the fulfilment of
His purpose in the revelation of Himself and the
redemption of man. It is with the distinctively
Christian conception of God and man in mutual
relation that we now approach the subject of this
study on Society, State and Church.

(1) IF the Christian conception of God—the most adequate for the mind and the most satisfying for the heart of man—is that of social personality, and if man's history is a revelation of the eternal reality of God in time as Father, Son, and Holy Spirit, then we must think of man as made in God's image as also social personality; but as creature in contrast with God as Creator. Man has the capacity for, but not the content of society in his own personality; he can realise his social personality only in relation to other persons endowed as he himself is. If it be said that man might realise himself as social in his relation to God, it may be maintained in opposition to the mystic definition of religion as " the flight of the alone to the Alone," and the modern corresponding one that " religion is what man does with his solitariness," that God's reality, however immediate the consciousness of communion may be, is never altogether unmediated, but God comes and gives Himself to man in nature and history. The message of the Hebrew prophets was mediated to them by the Divine

Providence in the course of their national history; and Wordsworth found in the beauty of Nature " the presence that disturbed him with the joy of elevated thoughts." A close examination of the revelations which the mystics claimed to have received in visions and voices discloses their dependence on the dogmas of the Church. Even Jesus in His teaching shows the mediation of the Old Testament revelation, of the sights and sounds of Nature, of the works and ways of man in His understanding of His Father, intimate as was His communion as Son. God is not Alone, and man is not alone in religious experience. How empty and often sordid solitariness even for communion with God, apart from social relations, can become the records of hermits have shown. Even in his relation to God man is normal as he is social, and as his solitude with God is conditioned by his relations with his fellow-men in society.

(2) If this truth is to be recognised even in man's communion with God, it can be confirmed from human life in all its aspects; and we may begin at what seems to be the furthest remove from his religion—namely, his kinship with the other animals, and his dependence on nature.

(a) In the preceding chapter stress was laid on man's superiority to the rest of living creatures as at the summit of the creative evolution, as shown in his distinctive human equipment in contrast to his animal inheritance. That truth does not need to be modified, but complementary facts must be recognised. As an animal, apart from his human equipment, man is in a more perilous and less favourable position for self-preservation and self-protection than the "humbler creation." For warfare with natural foes he has not the same armaments of horn and tusk, tooth and claw; for flight he has not the same swiftness as horse or deer; his naked body is exposed to the rigours of winter as are not the fur-clothed beasts; he cannot wing his way to a warmer clime as can birds. Nature would have defeated him in the struggle for existence, had his human gifts of mind not afforded more than a bare compensation for the lack of what other animals possess. Not least of his advantages is his capacity for forming and developing ever more intimate social relations. He is biologically a gregarious animal, but his sociality can reach far out beyond any gregariousness. Ants, bees and beavers display a gregariousness in a marvel of co-operation, but that co-operation has limits set to it by instinct, while man can expand it by his reason.

(*b*) If in some ways instinct seems more unerring than reason, its rigid frontiers are quickly reached. A woman errs in the care of her babe as the cat does not; but she can learn incalculably more of mother-craft than can a cat.

Thus reason transforms gregariousness into that social solidarity, that planned and ordered mutual aid and common enterprise, which have given us our culture and civilisation. How much does man's progress owe to his ability to speak and to write! Doubtless animals have means of communication with one another; a mother-hen can call her brood to the shelter of her wings. But as far as our observation allows a conclusion, no animals have such means of communication as will allow any progress in their habits such as is possible to man. Language is a product of society, and as regards range and content depends on the social development.

(c) Attention has been called, in opposition to an extravagant misunderstanding of Darwin's idea of " the struggle for existence," to the abundant evidences of mutual dependence in Nature of plant and animal life, the *symbiosis*, as it has been called, with which the science of *echology* is concerned; and even to what at least appears as altruism, care for another's life, even parental affection. The mating and the caring for offspring of birds appear to an appreciative imagination a romance of love. How much or how little sensibility accompanies the instinctive actions we cannot tell. At least this is true, that Nature has a kindlier aspect than Huxley's contrast between the cosmic process and human progress would indicate. Man's highest endowment, which the Christian revelation proclaims to be also God's, is love. Whether sex-relations began in promiscuity, as some anthropologists assert, and others as confidently deny, at some time sex-attraction acquired permanence, and the institution of marriage came to be. If the recognition of kinship through the mother (the matriarchate) preceded kinship though the father (the patriarchate) then the tender affection of mother and child came even earlier than the tender affection between man and woman, and the family came even before marriage was a recognised institution. This course of development seems to me less likely than that from the beginning the attraction of one man for one woman, which has been so beneficent, and yet also so destructive a factor in human history, belongs to man's original equipment, and that common care for offspring may go further back than the habits of some savage tribes have led some anthropologists to conclude. The long-continued helpessness of the human child, demanding such common care over the years, as other animals do not, is a decisive evidence of man's need of society for his self-protection and self-preservation. In this regard of man's progress as social personality it can be said: " a little child shall lead them." It is in the family—husband and wife, parent and child—

that a natural function, common to man and animal, is "sublimated" into a human affection, the basis of society.

(*d*) The family expands into the tribe under the same necessity of society for the achievement of human ends; and here "common blood" is assumed as the sacred bond, although an alien may be received by a solemn rite into "blood brotherhood." For varied reasons, tribes become allied and at last fused as nations; although common blood, or even common language, is no necessary factor in the formation of a nation, for which many historical causes can be traced, the myth of "blood" is sometimes maintained, as in Germany to-day. When one nation subdues another nation, and holds it in subjection without the assimilation to which a nation is due, there arises the empire, as of Egypt, Assyria, Babylon, Persia, Greece, Rome.

(3) I have laid such stress on man's need of society to counter what seems to me to be a present danger of reactionary thinking. It would seem as if in human thought, as in emotion, there were a law of ebb and flow, the rise and the fall of opinions—the movement between two extremes. The Corn-Law rhymer, Ebenezer Elliott, wrote of Socialism:—

> What is a Socialist? One who has yearnings
> For equal division of unequal earnings;

Idler or bungler, or both, he is willing
To fork out his penny and pocket your shilling.

Sir Wm. Vernon Harcourt, the Liberal statesman, said, with a rhetorical exaggeration: " We are all Socialists now," meaning that there was a movement, even in Liberalism, which had stood for individual liberty, to a recognition of social obligations; and it must never be forgotten in the depressed condition of the Liberal Party to-day how much Liberalism when in power did to secure social reform, government *for* as well as *by* the people. The Nationalist Government, disavowing Socialism, has not only been compelled by public opinion to pass more social legislation than its professed principles would have led one to expect, but has even done more to bring industry and commerce under Government control than any previous one, and has, though from other motives and for other ends, made the governmental machinery, which a Labour Government could adopt and adapt for its policy. Thus has the tide risen. The perils which the " totalitarian," *omnicompetent, omnipotent* State in Germany especially now threatens is bringing about in some minds a fall. A leader of one of the Nonconformist churches pleaded for a return to the faith of the Nonconformist fathers, and even their " slogan ": " A free Church in a free State." A leader of another maintained that we must go back to the old Liberalism, even to *laissez-faire* principles. It is not a vain conjecture that even leaders in the churches may prove " blind guides of the blind," and may try to reverse the movement in the churches to a fuller recognition of the claims of, and the duties to society which Christian love demands, and for which the present world crisis urgently and imperatively calls. There is a safe course which can be steered between the Scylla of *laissez-faire*, and the Charybdis of the totalitarian State, and that course this volume will endeavour to chart.

(4) The necessity of society to man has not always been fully recognised, even although one of the world's classics, Plato's *Republic*, assumes an analogy between the man and the society, and strives to see the microcosm in the light of the macrocosm.

(*a*) The seventeenth and eighteenth centuries, in which mathematical and physical conceptions prevailed in science, had a *mechanical* view of society. The individual was a unit in himself, and society was a sum of such units, externally related; society was imposed on nature; so Hobbes and Rousseau.

(*b*) At the beginning of the nineteenth century Auguste Comte brought the study of society into the hierarchy of the sciences under the hybrid title of *sociology*, which he justified on the ground

D

that in it must be combined the speculative genius of Greece and the practical ethos of Rome. As in all the other sciences, sociology, although it was the crown of *Positive Philosophy*, must deal solely with social phenomena in their resemblances, co-existences and sequences; this positive method he contrasted with as superseding the metaphysical and the theological of philosophy and religion and yet in his *Positive Polity* he had to provide as motive of action the Religion of Humanity. Sociology came next to biology in greater complexity. When Herbert Spencer applied to society the analogy of the organism, he did not advance beyond a fundamentally mechanical view, since he assumed that the categories of physics could be applied in biology, the general principle of differentiation and integration. The body grows, so does society; the body survives amid the changes of its constituent cells, so society continues while the generations pass; as increased complexity of structure in the body involves increased dependence of all the parts on the whole, so the division of labour in society in its advance requires greater co-operation. (I am to some extent paraphrasing to make his analogy more intelligible.) For him, however, the individual is still the social unit, and hence he disappoints a legitimate expectation by his relapse into *laissez-faire*; as only individuals can experience pleasure

or pain, individual interests should not be sacrificed to a supposed common good. Other
writers have drawn the proper inference from this
analogy in maintaining that individual interests
cannot thus be detached from the common good,
as St. Paul does, when developing the same
analogy, he insists that the members of the
church suffer or rejoice together (I Cor. xii. 26).

(c) J. S. Mackenzie in his book *An Introduction
to Social Philosophy*, which still deserves study,
accepts the analogy of the organism, but develops
it not from the standpoint of physical science, but
of idealist philosophy. It is as rational subjects
that men have intrinsic relations to one another,
need a rational environment, and contribute
in their individual development to social
progress.

R. M. Maciver in his book *Community*, *a
Sociological Study*, to which I assign exceptional
value, rejects the analogy of the organism in
relation to society, as an explanation which is
more obscure than what it seeks to explain. He
substitutes the conception of *Community*, but
rejects the assumption of Durkheim and Mc-
Dougall (the psychic view) that a union of minds
is a *mind*. Society " lacks the integrity, isolation
and unity of volition which are essential to mind;
and the influence which society exercises on
individual minds does not prove that it is a

supermind." [1] In the whole range of human personality men have common motives, interests, purposes, activities; this community is the social bond. A natural relation, such as sexual intercourse, or the begetting and bearing of offspring, does not constitute society, although it is a physical basis for it; there must be a conscious common interest and a consequent common volition; a society is a *willed* relation. A flock, or a herd, or a pack is not a society. Where men have common interests, or community, they will come together in an *association*, and that association will have common modes of action, which are its *institutions*. This terminology of Maciver I think it is convenient to adopt to give precision to our exposition. We may apply it to the two subjects with which in this volume we are concerned, the Church and the State. What makes the Church a community is the common possession (Koinōnia) of the Holy Spirit, the new life from God which results from faith in the love of God as realised in the grace of Christ. The Church (*ecclesia*, the called out) is the *association* in which this community brings believers together, the ministry, the worship and the witness, the sacraments are the *institutions* in which the

[1] See my own book *The Christian Ideal for Human Society*, p. 283, in the Introduction of Part IV of which these theories are discussed.

association functions. As regards the State, the community is the common nationality, the sense of belonging to one nation, a conception which is so complex that it will need at a later stage to be much more fully discussed. The State itself is the *association* of individual subjects or citizens, and the *institutions* are monarchy, parliament, law-courts, etc.

(*d*) While agreeing with Maciver in his rejection of the *psychic* theory, which savours of mythology, he seems to me not to recognise adequately the unity of thought, feeling, will, or interest, aspiration, ideal, which emerges from the union not of minds, but of persons in the whole range of personality. Something emerges which is more than the sum of the persons composing the society. The individual is not absorbed into the society, and yet he is taken up into a larger life than his own in " its integrity, isolation, and unity of volition." *Esprit de corps*, *Zeitgeist*, team-spirit are not mere phrases, products of individual minds: they in turn affect those minds, may even possess and dominate them. Maciver recognises that the fundamental law of progress is this: " Socialisation and individualisation are the two sides of a single process; sociality and individuality develop *pari passu*." [1] When the individual is

---

[1] *Op. cit.*, p. 173.

fully developed in his individuality his socialisation will be completed also. Does that not mean that his sense of *union* with others will be raised to a sense of the *unity* of the society? Where there is love, and in the measure in which there is love, there is common life, which transcends and transforms the individual lives so united, as in marriage. It is possible that it is only in religious community, because it is the common possession of the Holy Spirit, that social unity can be most fully realised. A common life with God gives a transcendent unity to the common life of man in God, as the relation of God to man, and man to God is much more immediate and intimate than can be the relation of individual men to one another, unless in so far as they share that common life in God. Without any claim that the words are the *ipsissima verba* of Jesus, how significant and valuable is the witness of the spiritual genius, to whom we owe the Fourth Gospel. " The glory which thou hast given me I have given unto them; that they may be one even as we are one; I in them and thou in me, that they may be perfected into one, that the world may know that thou didst send me, and lovedst them as thou hast loved me " (John xvii. 22, 23). *Perfected into one:* social unity the end of personal perfection. The Church so divided does not realise that unity and its authority and influence in the world is less than it might be. Were the Spirit of God, through the Church, to pervade, purify and perfect all social relations, then we might look for a human society on earth that reflected the glory of the one God, Father, Son and Holy Spirit, "the loving, the loved, the love."

(5) What are the *objects* for which society as a *willed* relation exists? What are the sources of the *community* which is the motive of the *associations* of men as functioning through *institutions*? The fundamental needs and impulses on which the continuance of the race depends have already been mentioned—the family, which gives permanence to the relation of man and woman, parent and child.

(*a*) Man is dependent for the provision of his bodily needs on Nature, the *material* objects which he must appropriate and adapt by his labour. Man is exposed to the dangers and suffering which physical forces may inflict upon him, and he must use means for protecting himself. The provision of needs, the protection against dangers or sufferings, may be both comprehended under the term, *the conquest of Nature*. Natural laws must be known by his science, so that physical forces may be directed and controlled by his strength, and still more his skill, so as to be beneficent and not injurious. That conquest we may also describe as civilisation. That process has been carried far, and very rapid has been the progress within living memory. A book appeared in the nineteenth century under the title *The Wonderful Century*, but the first three decades of the seventeenth century would justify for its record the description, *The More Wonderful Century*: that conquest is by no means complete, and, Nature and man being what they are, can never be complete. Disease and death still baffle man's endeavour. There are natural catastrophes, which man cannot prevent, such as earthquakes, volcano, tempest, but he may learn how to escape some, if not all, these evils. Over flood, famine, plague he can gain a larger measure of mastery. Yet it is an idle boast that he can so exercise dominion over Nature as to become altogether " master of his fate, and captain of his soul." He can, it is true, by the culture of his personality gain such an attitude even to the dangers and the sufferings Nature inflicts on him as to retain his spiritual independence of all outward things. It is so evident that it needs but to be mentioned that this progress would have been impossible had there not been a corresponding advance in society to secure general and effective corporate action. No man, no nation, no race can on the level of present civilisation be isolated. Science, industry, commerce, all involve a world-wide interdependence. Even for the conquest of Nature mankind is becoming a community, although it has but inadequately secured the corresponding necessary associations and institutions.

(b) Material civilisation has rapidly got ahead of personal culture, using the word culture to include not intellectual development only, but the development of personality. In gaining mastery over Nature, mankind generally has not gained self-mastery in corresponding measure. No doubt there are men and women who, still imperfect, have advanced far along the path to perfection; and they are the light of the world and the salt of the earth. But this highest type of culture has not yet proved itself the mustard seed of the expanding plant, or the leaven of the transformed meal of society. Man is physical, intellectual, æsthetic, moral, social, religious, and his culture should embrace a proportionate development so that he can present a symmetrical type of manhood. *Mens sana in corpore sano* is a sound maxim, a safe guide, if we understand by *mens* more than the intellect. It may be that no man can realise that ideal perfectly, that the price of excellence in one of his personal functions must be the neglect of others; was Darwin's inability to appreciate poetry too high a price for his concentration on science? It may be that, as members of society, individuals need to be complementary to one another: and yet must concentration on one function, however necessary, and valuable socially, involve the exclusion of other interests and activities? Should not a man try, as far as he can, to be a microcosm in himself, even if he must be a brain, a hand, a fact in the body of society, the macrocosm? The good of society as a whole will depend on the quality of its members, their wholeness as persons. Hence education as the means of developing personality must not be measured by utilitarian standards, by technical or professional efficiency. The day school has something more and better to do than to furnish business men with smart office-boys or girls, or farmers with good ploughmen or dairy-maids. That education may at a certain stage be given a utilitarian interest need not be denied; but the notion that education must be determined by the station of the parents, or the vocation of the child is a pernicious error. Society, for the common good, cannot afford to have " mute, inglorious Miltons or village Hampdens," but must generously and impartially offer the tools of culture to all who can handle them. It is desirable that the social ranks should be to a large extent recruited from below, to use, without approving, the current terms.

(c) Important as physical, intellectual and æsthetic culture are—and only a narrow moralism, or a shallow pietism would depreciate and neglect them—yet more important is man's moral, social and religious culture; although we may distinguish them, we must not separate them. Without entering on a discussion of the question whether man has duties to himself or to God, which I believe he has, we may affirm that it is in his social relations that a man's morality finds its broadest field of exercise. Love to God is the motive, and love of self the measure of love of the neighbour; as in Christianity this love is the highest principle, we may recognise that, for its own protection, preservation and progress, society must secure the right social relations of all its members through religion. It is interested in the character and the faith of its members as these help or hinder the quality of these relations; but in the highest expressions of the moral conscience and the religious consciousness there should be the utmost individual liberty and responsibility which these social relations allow. Goodness and godliness are a vital interest of society, and social relations should not prevent, but promote these; but excellence here cannot be directed and controlled by society; but must be left to the " self-knowledge, self-reverence, and self-control," of the cultured personality. Men cannot be made good or godly by Act of Parliament: but right social relations demand and justify their being kept sober, clean, honest, and truthful. While there has been some progress as regards the quality of social relations, that progress has fallen very far short of the advance in civilization or in physical, intellectual and æsthetic culture. Social relations have not yet been adequately adjusted to economic conditions. The present world distress is due not to insufficient wealth to meet need, not even solely to the maladjustment within the economic structure of society, although that is serious, and unaltered threatens ruin; but it is largely in that maladjustment due not only to wrong social relations, but even to false theories as to what these relations should be. Until the falsity of these theories is recognised, and the relations are corrected the evils will continue. This is an anticipation of what in subsequent chapters will need to be very much more fully developed, but it may be mentioned here to illustrate how necessary to the security, prosperity and progress of any society it is that the truth be discovered about, and so the right be asserted in, social relations. All the objectives of society just discussed are mutually dependent.

(6) It is because society has failed to function adequately and properly in securing these three objectives that there are the difficulties, dangers, distress and despondency which fill the world to-day, and justify the description of the situation without any exaggeration as the world-crisis: the only certainty is that the issue of the present

conditions is altogether uncertain, whether it will be recovery or ruin. Even for those who have faith in the providence of God in human history, confidence that God will fulfil His purpose of goodness and grace to the children of men, there is the question whether, unless a remedy is found for the world's disease, the ultimate salvation may not involve incalculably great sacrifices. Another war might not end civilisation, as is often prophesied, but certainly its consequences would be as much more terrible than those of the last war as the resources of destruction brought into exercise would exceed those of which mankind has had tragic experience.

(a) As I have written at some length on this crisis in my book entitled *Can Christ Save Society?* I refrain from any fuller discussion here, and content myself with briefly stating only those considerations which are necessary for the exposition of my present subject. Mackenzie, in the book already referred to, states that modern society since the Fall of the Roman Empire has passed through three phases: (i) the *subjugation* of the barbarous tribes to some measure of civilisation and culture, morals and religion by the Christian Church, which preserved, although imperfectly, the treasures of the Ancient World, and transmitted them to the Modern; (ii) the *emancipation* which in the Renaissance and the

Reformation and subsequent movements cast off the yoke of the Mediæval World which had become too galling; (iii) the *organisation*, needed to replace the superseded order, and to save liberty from licence, in reconciling individual interests with the common good. This process has not yet been adequately carried through, and the cause of the present world situation is due to the failure to organise society so that its associations and institutions may be adapted to the ever-changing conditions, material and mental.

(*b*) As we look around, we see a world disorganised, or wrongly organised. The economic system, to give the more crucial instances, is not organised so that the abundant wealth of the world, actual and potential, may fully meet the still-abounding wants of men, and thus the tragic parodox of *poverty and plenty* may be ended. In the political sphere democracy has failed to be so organised as to secure the full benefits of government *of* the people *by* the people *for* the people, and thus to exclude the humiliating illusion of the advantage of dictatorship. In the international sphere the nations also have shown themselves less organised for the promotion of peace than for the pursuit of war, so that there is ever the dangerous confusion of professions of peace and preparations for war. The needs of mankind are not being met, their hopes fulfilled, their aims

accomplished, as with the world's present resources appears altogether possible.

(c) A faith which energised in the works by
which the possible ideal might become actual is
lacking, for man's goodwill falls far short of the
present demands. Liberty has not secured equality because there has been a lack of fraternity.
If the Church could inspire the faith, the State
might effect the works; but because there is a
severance between the faith and the works, the
Church is failing to fulfil its mission, and the State
to discharge its functions in such a way as to
assure, not ruin, but recovery in the world's
crisis. The situation to-day in some lands is
even worse. Instead of the co-operation of Church
and State, each recognising its opportunities and
obligations in its distinctive sphere, there is even
conflict, as there has often been in the past, because they are often thought of as rivals, and not
allies, and mutually suspect one another of tres-
pass. That there may be co-operation and not
conflict, it is necessary to define the functions of
the State and the mission of the Church. To
prevent a relapse to subjugation, to make the
emancipation sure and safe, to organise the varied
and complex interests and activities of individuals,
classes, nations, races, for the advance and not the
hindrance of the progressive universal good of
mankind, the Church must inspire the motive and

the standard, the State provide the means and the methods of this building of " the New Jerusalem," not only in " England's fair and pleasant land," but in all lands—not a Utopia, but a Eutopia, an earthly city fashioned after the pattern of the heavenly.

(1) IN the previous chapter the State was described as an *association*, constituted to give effect to a community, the nation. Family and tribe are narrower associations within the nation; but we can begin our discussion with the nation.

(*a*) What is a nation? The etymology does not lead us to the definition, as the nation does not correspond with the native, *born* in the same country, or of the same blood. A nation has "a local habitation and a name"; it has its own territory with frontiers severing it from other nations, but not all its subjects or citizens have been born within that territory, and they may retain their connection even if they wander afar. One country may claim those born within it as belonging to the nation; another may regard naturalisation as a special privilege to be acquired after a fixed period of residence.

(*b*) Only a tribe or a people, remote from the human currents in a world, in which there are now no entirely closed lands, could claim to be of one blood, one natural stock. Most of the

E

nations of Europe have many strains of blood mingled in their native population, to say nothing of the strangers within their gates. The claim being made in Germany at the present hour, which would be comic in view of its history as a nation, is proving tragic in its consequences, the exclusion of the Non-Aryan or Semitic (Jewish) inhabitants from the full privileges of citizenship, and even in many cases their persecution. Where there is difference of colour, the mixture of blood is more apparent; and the desirable realisation of national unity is being hindered by the " colour bar." The United States of America and South Africa are cursed with this prejudice about blood; in the caste system of India in relation to the outcastes this same difference of physical descent is proving a real difficulty in making valid the claim of national unity. In Great Britain there is a very mixed population—Celtic, Saxon, Danish, Norman, etc., in ancestry; yet there is national unity. Such distinction as there is between Wales and Scotland on the one hand and England on the other is only partially due to natural descent, and mainly to history. While Welshman and Scotsman object to being called English, they are merged without any difficulty in the national unity of Great Britain. Canada, Australia, and South Africa claim to be nations, independent

States, and yet they recognise a common kinship (some reservation being made for the African Dutch). Recent developments in the relation of nations within the British Empire show that the separation in the local habitation does modify the sense of unity due to such feeling of kinship. In the United States of America there is, as the name indicates, a federation of States, and yet in recent years there has been a tendency to recognise common interests as demanding a greater unity of corporate action. It is interesting to note that it is a President of the Democratic Party, the tradition of which is the independence of the States, who is doing more than any previous one has done to advance this process of unification. A nation is there in the making out of the most diverse racial elements which have ever been brought together. Not all American citizens are 100 per cent. American, or possess the sense of national unity.

(*c*) Language, with the literature to which it offers access, is a potent national bond, and is of higher quality than " blood," for it belongs to man as personal, as mind in the widest sense. There can be no doubt that, despite political divisions in separate states, the English-speaking world has a unity which many nations do not possess, because the language opens the door to a treasure-house of a common culture, for the excellence of which, without any partiality, a very high claim can be made. Nevertheless, as has often been pointed out, the common language may deceive as to the closeness of the affinity, and the wholeness of the community between Great Britain and the States; and a unity of interest and purpose may be assumed where it does not exist. We in Great Britain may irritate our American friends by presuming agreement where they may differ, and they may disappoint our expectations; thus there may be some misunderstanding, and even estrangement. Nevertheless it is a fact of great significance and even promise for mankind that Great Britain, which sends her sons and daughters to the ends of the earth, and the United States, which gathers its people from the ends, are linked by this bond of common speech. Switzerland is a nation where difference of language does not destroy the national unity, and yet there are other differences along with that of the language which leave the sense of unity less complete than it might be with one speech.

(d) As has been already suggested in dealing with language, it is a common culture with a common history as its antecedent which makes a nation one more than do one soil, one blood, one speech, although these factors must also be recognised in the history. As a historical factor a common religion may unite, and difference of religion may divide. Ireland is a conspicuous example. Scotland as a nation owes a great deal to its dominant Presbyterians; and Anglican episcopacy wounds national sentiment in asserting the inferiority of that ecclesiastical type. In Germany it is true Roman Catholic and Protestant are alike patriotic; but it must not be forgotten that Roman Catholicism, through its effective unity in the Centre Party, exercised more influence in politics than would ordinarily fall to a minority. One of the dangers of granting, and the difficulties of working self-government in India will be the antagonism of Hindu and Moslem. With difference of religion go other differences; moral standards, educational demands, even in many cases economic conditions vary with the religion. Hence the minorities in Europe, who desire to preserve their national unity, demand the use of their mother tongue, the observance of their own religious worship, the provision of an education for their children corresponding to their language and religion.

(e) A nation can in the process of history be formed, if peoples of diverse descent can be *assimilated* in a common culture, language, religion, morals, and education, the personal as contrasted with the natural conditions; and the English nation is a conspicuous instance of such assimilation, for it has not been made by absorption by one dominant people of all the others. The Norman Conquest did not make England Norman; English law does not derive its principles from Roman; the English language —surely one of the richest organs for expression which the world knows and fitted to be a world-language by its grammatical simplicity, but not its confusing pronunciation where the sounds have no invariable correspondence with the signs— combined Celtic, Saxon, Danish, and Norman elements, as well as the contribution of the classical languages. The names of natural features are largely Celtic; the names of the oldest towns and villages Saxon, and in some parts of the country Danish; the Saxon herdsman kept the names of his charges unchanged, ox, sheep, deer; but the Norman lord gave their flesh the Norman names, beef, mutton, venison.

(f) Where a minority resists assimilation most is when it is forced by the majority, or when it is conscious of its superiority in civilisation and culture. Germans are galled by their subjection to Poland, and Magyars by Rumanian domination. For world peace it is not desirable that these minorities should maintain their intransigence; it would be well if there could be assimilation. For no European frontier could now be changed without some injustice and some danger of war, and the multiplication of small nations adds confusion to a divided world. The number of the peoples under alien rule is now smaller than it was, as the emancipation of peoples subjected in the three Empires of Russia, Germany and Austria-Hungary was an act of historical justice. In fixing frontiers, however, the principle of the self-determination of nations was applied not impartially, but with a bias in favour of the peoples whom the Allied Powers had attached to themselves as opponents of the great Empire. Not a forced assimilation, for that is a method that defeats its purpose, but a gradual and voluntary would be a wiser and better solution of the problem than rectification of frontiers, unless in a few cases of flagrant injustice and injury.

(2) The War has let loose a dangerous, fanatical nationalism, which is making the international machinery for peace much less effective than it might be.

(a) It has become a religion, if not superseding, yet perverting the religion professed. A common orthodoxy is far less potent to unite than nationalism to divide the Balkan peoples. Some " German Christians " are more German than Christian, even when they have not adopted the " German-Faith " movement instead of Christianity. Religious sanctions are being invoked for this national arrogance and exclusiveness. The claim for the superiority of Germandom (the word must be coined, for no other will quite express the idea) over " the lesser breeds without the law " (a German *nomos* which may challenge the Christian ethics is asserted) is based on the alleged creative decree of God. If, as the first chapter has shown, God is not only Creator, Preserver, and Ruler, but also Father of all without distinction of race or nation, if in Christ the differences which divide men are transcended in the recognition of a common redeemed humanity, such a notion can be dismissed as a pagan myth. On historical grounds the much-despised, reviled and even persecuted Jew can advance a higher claim to belong to God's chosen people, for Germany, with all its values for other nations, has made no such distinctive contribution to the kingdom of God as has Judæa.

(*b*) But this whole mode of thinking is crude. The Hebrew prophets did trace the divine providence in the history of their nation; and Jesus has taught us to trust the Heavenly Father who feeds the birds, clothes the flowers, notes every sparrow's fall, and counts the hairs of our head. But this Divine presence, interest and activity is in and by the natural order and the historical progress. Just as Bacon and Descartes were right in insisting that conjectures as to the design of

God in natural phenomena must not take the place of enquiry as to phenomenal causes, and so secured freedom for physical science from theological incursions, so also it is necessary to view historical events in their historical antecedents, to trace an unbroken continuity of moral order, men reaping as they sow, and only then to discover the divine providence not in any breaks in the process, but in the character of the process as a whole. To invoke divine agency for our preferences, and Satanic for our prejudices is to short-circuit thought, with disastrous results for our understanding history, and our insight into God's works and ways with men. We may reverently and gratefully recognise that the British Empire has a significance and value for the Divine Providence, presenting an opportunity to, and imposing an obligation on the peoples who are included in it, to use their resources for the furtherance and not the hindrance of the Divine purpose, but this does not justify any arrogant claim to be Heaven's favourites. The words of the Hebrew prophet are as applicable to-day as ever to any nation which claims to be privileged by God. "You only have I known of all the families of the earth: therefore will I visit on you all your iniquities" (Amos iii. 2). God elects to service and to sacrifice, and not to advantage over other nations. His creative decrees, of which we know nothing unless as nature and history disclose them, are subordinate to His redemptive purpose for all mankind.

(c) There seems to me to be a close connection between this irrational nationalism and acquiescence in dictatorships. The nation becomes incarnated in the leader, through whom it believes that its aims will be accomplished and its hopes fulfilled. Sun-Yat-Sen in China, Lenin in Russia, Mussolini in Italy and Hitler in Germany are receiving the kind of worship that the Roman Empire gave the Emperor. Admiration and adulation of their leader is an outlet for this hysterical mood. A nation that raises itself over other nations will readily exalt one leader, who promises to satisfy its ambitions, over all other organs of self-government. That violence has been used to establish and maintain this leadership does not disprove this legitimate inference from the history, for the violence would not have been so easily successful had there not been a hypnotised nation. In our own country the word "National" has had the same effect on many of the citizens, who give an unreasoning acquiescence to a policy which without this spell might have been doubted or questioned;

patriotism seems to demand a suspension of critical scrutiny.

As regards one of these instances, Lenin in Russia—a qualification may seem necessary. It may be said that it is not *nationalism* which animates the rulers of Russia, but belief in, and zeal for an economic system. But the direction of that zeal, and the methods which it inspires are Russian, and can be traced back to the pre-war conditions in Russia. In all these nationalisms there is an exasperation against existing conditions. Czarism is responsible for Bolshevism; a futile party strife for Fascism; the oppression and humiliation to which Germany was subjected after and since the War for Nazidom. Before we judge any movement we must consider its antecedents. Some lines of Schiller may be recalled:

> " 'Fore slaves, when they their fetters break,
> Before free men need no man quake."

In all these dangerous nationalisms Europe is reaping what it has sown.

(*d*) The interests of the nation, however conceived, become the dominant, almost the exclusive motives of action; all other interests must be subordinated to the one interest, or even sacrificed for it. As the State is the organ of national action, the sovereignty of the State becomes absolute, and it can do as it will with all other associations; hence the " totalitarian " conception of the State; it must direct and control the " total " activities of the community and all these must be brought into *conformity* (*Gleichschaltung*) with its character. It is significant, however, that it is the Church alone which in Germany is refusing to be brought into that *totality*, to be shaped by that *conformity*. To this conflict we shall return in a later chapter; but it seemed necessary at this point to show some of the results of an extreme nationalism.

(*e*) Before we pass to deal with the functions of the State we must ask, What is the Christian judgment on nationalism? Such nationalisms as have been described must be unreservedly condemned, and we shall have occasion to state that condemnation in detail. This does not involve, however, that patriotism, or love of country, people, speech, is inconsistent with Christian universalism, which does not abolish all the differences that divide men, but so sublimates some that they need not divide. Slavery Christianity has condemned as inconsistent with the value of personality; but sex it has transformed in the Christian ideal of marriage, and in like manner it preserves nationality in internationalism, and does not merge it in cosmopolitanism. Without appealing to creative decrees, about which we can only pretend to know, we may say that the course of history as the process of the divine providence justifies us in believing that at present at least the differences of nations are not inconsistent with the universal redemptive purpose of God.

(3) This extended treatment of the subject of the nation is not a digression, but a necessary introduction to our conception of the State, for the State is the organ of nationality; the community which makes the nation one has as its association for corporate action the State.

(*a*) Whether the State was decreed by God before or after the Fall is one of those futile questions which theology is not competent to answer; but as the State has been described as decreed by God as a restraint of sin by the exercise of force, that false conception may be repudiated. We cannot pretend to know what a sinless development of mankind would have been, but trying to understand the actual course of history, we are justified at least in assuming as our working hypothesis that it is just as normal for men to associate themselves because of their community of interests and purposes in tribes and in nations as in families. Anarchy and sinlessness do not seem to be complementary notions, nor government and sin. Men living and working together would in all cases need some kind of social order, some regulation of their mutual relations; regular co-ordination is necessary to effective co-operation. Because of man's sinfulness, the State may appear as having as its main (if not sole) function the restraint of wickedness by force: but in the modern rationalised and moralised State provision for the common good is becoming more prominent than protection against common danger or injury. The sentiment of patriotism which is the support of the State in discharging its functions is probably itself the subjective response to the objective reality of the State.

(b) If the State, then, is not solely or even mainly punitive, but serviceable for the common good, it is quite false to regard force as its distinctive activity. It must prescribe laws to be obeyed, it must establish an order to be maintained, so that its citizens or subjects may pursue their individual vocations, undisturbed and uninjured by the lawless and disorderly, whom it may need to restrain by force; but criminals are an exception, and the community as a whole goes on in its ways and works, not conscious of any oppression, and not even conscious of the protection which it is receiving. As in the relations of nations, force may be used in war to resist aggression, or injury to national interests, so in the relations of the members of a society force may be used to prevent or punish crime: but as little in the one case as in the other is force the only, or the chief resource of the State; it is increasingly recognised as the last resort. The conscience of civilised nations is condemning war, and is insisting that in the treatment of crime even remedial or reformatory methods are to displace merely punitive. If it be urged that force is always in the background, it can be replied that in the measure in which a nation becomes civilised and cultured does the authority of the State depend less and less on the threat of force, and more and more on the free consent of citizens.

(c) To hold that God wills the State to be punitive of sin by force, is to justify the policy being pursued in Italy and Germany as the most conspicuous instances. To hold, on the other hand, that a State which by its beneficent activities in the service of the community can so rely on the loyal support of its citizens that its use of force can be restricted to the prevention of crime only, can be regarded as an agent of God's redemptive purpose, is to have a standard of judgment of the State itself. As long as mankind has not been fully brought under the constraints of grace, the restraints of law are necessary, but as a " tutor unto Christ " these restraints should be made not only deterrent but educative and conciliating. We must rid ourselves of the pernicious inheritance of the past that the Christian by faith in God and love for his neighbour must live as purely and helpfully as he can in an order of society which he has no means or hope of changing and in some measure conforming to the will of God in Christ (the Lutheran doctrine); but we must with courage and confidence declare that whether under historical conditions the Kingdom of God can and will be fully manifested on earth or not, yet in some measure, and in a progressive way, the kingdoms of this world can be brought into obedience to the Kingdom of the Son of God's Love—a view which at the Stockholm Conference was condemned by some of the Germans present as Anglo-American activism.

(d) Whether, as many fear, we have entered on a period of reaction, in which conflicting interests, Communist or Fascist, will try to seize the reins of government, and seek by violence to destroy or to preserve the existing social order or not, we can in this country hope to pass through the inevitable social transition without conflict, and the Christian Church at least must steadfastly oppose any policy of violence, and exercise a ministry of reconciliation, so that the ideal of the State which has been above suggested may displace the actuality as it is being experienced in so many lands, giving so poignant an interest to the questions of the relation of Church and State. Believing as I do, that conflict in that relation is not necessary, and that co-operation is possible, I should urge that we do not approach the discussion of the functions of the State in an attitude of suspicion, as though it were an enemy to be feared, but in a spirit of confidence because it can be won as an ally of the Church. While it would be explicable if Nonconformists, with the memory of persecution by the State, were to desire to keep Church and State apart " A free Church in a free State," I shall try to show that the functions of the State have been so extended and the mission of the Church, as it ought to be conceived, has been so expanded that apartness is now impossible.

(4) Abstract definitions of the functions of the State apart from the actual conditions of any nation have no value. As the State is the organ of the corporate activity of the nation to give effect to its common interests and purposes, its functions will vary not only with these common interests and purposes, but also

F

with the possibility and the desirability of such corporate action. A State where scarcity prevails cannot command the resources of one where plenty abounds. Some general considerations may, however, be offered. I cannot commit myself to either of the extreme views, *individualism*, which aims at reducing corporate action to a minimum or *collectivism*, which desires that action at a maximum.

(*a*) As one who believes in the value and the sacredness of personality, I should desire the exercise of as wide a liberty as common interests allow, and the acceptance of as great a responsibility as the common needs demand. A man should measure his duties by his rights, and the social burdens he assumes by the social benefits he enjoys. Every man should bear his own burden according to his capacity, and should bear the burdens of others in proportion to his resources beyond that capacity (Gal. vi. 2, 5). He who freely receives from society should as freely give to it. Nay, Christian love would go further and render more service than it requires, even as the Son of Man came not to be served, but to serve (Mat. xx. 28).

(*b*) If any service of the community can be more efficiently and more economically rendered by corporate action than by individual enterprise, and if the State has the resources, it should

assume that service. If a choice had to be
made between economy and efficiency, efficiency
should have the preference, as in the long
run efficiency also proves itself economy. The
cry of private interests that public service is
not so good or so cheap as private can be dis-
counted, and has been in many cases disproved;
and it should not pass the wit of man to secure
as good management for a municipal gas works
as for a limited liability company's. A high
standard of personal integrity and public spirit
is necessary to exclude even from public services
all private interests. Where a service is a
necessity, such as water, gas, electricity, and by
its nature must be a monopoly, there seems to
be a still stronger case for corporate action. The
nature of the service must determine whether
the administration shall be national, or local,
or local with relation to national; *e.g.* it would
seem that the supply of water and the system of
drainage must cover a much wider area than
that of a local authority.

(*c*) One of the ways in which the unequal
distribution of wealth can be compensated for
is in the increase and improvement of the
public services. One way in which the defect
of the present economic system in failing to
provide regular employment can be corrected
is the undertaking of public works which will

meet a common need, add to the common wealth, and also provide employment. In the economic sphere it is folly and wrong to imagine that private interests have any moral right to command this rising tide of corporate action, national or municipal, to cease its flow : "thus far and no further." There are associations of employers who in their public utterances display a lack of wisdom, which it is to be hoped that they do not fall into in the conduct of their businesses. They hold that the action of the State is to be condemned when it is for the protection of, or the provision for, the working classes; their cry is "Keep you hands off—let us do what we please with our own." When, however, foreign competition is to be prevented, the State cannot give them too much protection. While the State must be impartial as between private interests, yet the consumer— the community as a whole—should have a prior claim to the producer, with, of course, the limitation that he must be left the means and the incentive to produce, for that also is the interest of the consumer. In the present crisis, when consumption (effective demand) is falling short of production and production has to be reduced, involving unemployment and waste of wealth, the State would be serving the interests of the producer in the long run, as well

as the interests of the consumer with regard
to his immediate needs, if it took steps to secure
a wider distribution of wealth, a more general
ability to buy the goods that are for sale, by
the means already mentioned, the public services and public works, but also by a limitation
of profits, as is already being done in a hap-
hazard way by the dealing in industrial shares,
by schemes of profit-sharing, by directing the
investment of capital to the industries which
will most benefit the community, by regulating
credit and currency in the public instead of the
private interests. I am not personally here
advocating any one of these methods as immediately practicable, as I am no believer in " Socialism in our own time," but a believer in " the
inevitableness of gradualness "; but I am mentioning these means as all in my judgment
within the competence of the State, whenever
and wherever the needs of the community for
this wider distribution of wealth to end this
paradox of *poverty amid plenty* may demand
and justify corporate action.

(*d*) Such extension of the corporate action of
the State has no terrors, for " Socialism will
not be the end of all things," as some dread,
but that extension should not take place simply
that an abstract theory of *collectivism* may find
general application, but only in so far as, and

when it can be shown that the good of the community as a whole is being sacrificed to private interests by the continuance of any enterprise without adequate public control, for there might be cases where control without ownership would suffice, and that the community would gain, and not lose, by a change. Such economic knowledge and such moral insight as I possess incline me towards individual liberty and responsibility even in the economic sphere, but my social sympathy, my compassion for human need and suffering, compel me to re- cognise the imperative necessity of increasing corporate action, the extension of the functions of the State. I have no such reservations as regards the social services; the State should promote the health of all; it should provide for the bodily needs of all, in so far as they or those on whom they have a claim cannot make adequate provision; it should secure equal educational opportunity for all, so that the tools should be in the hands of all who can use them; as has already been mentioned—water, gas, electricity, transport, communication (telegraphs, telephones, wireless) should be provided for all at lowest cost: the only limitation is that the common good requires, and the corporate action can provide better and cheaper service than private enterprise.

(e) As in all these forms of social service there is a danger of an unsympathetic, undiscerning officialism. Wherever and whenever practicable, there should be unofficial co-operation, service rendered not for a salary received, but from love for man: it is in this form that philanthropy must be exercised in the measure in which relief of need is taken over by the State. What is better still, is that men and women should enter the public services as a Christian vocation, constrained by the love of Christ to minister to the least of His brethren as unto Him (Matt. xxv. 40). There may in such public service be necessary limitations on direct Christian witness, as, for instance, an inquiry by a nurse into the spiritual condition of a dying patient; but there can be no limitation on the indirect Christian influence of loving ministry. It would be illegitimate, however, if propaganda of any kind, and not the purest philanthropy were the motive. To this subject we must return in Chapter VI.

(5) It is inevitable that the State should take the responsibility for the education of the people, not only intellectual, but also moral; and that it should concern itself about all the influences which effect character, for the State requires citizens intelligent and trustworthy. Literature, the theatre and the cinema are

agencies of improvement or corruption, and the State must exercise some control so that the morals of the community shall be protected against evil, and provided with good influences. How far censorship and control can in this regard go is a much disputed question, which we need not here attempt to answer.

(a) One of the burning questions of the recent past can, however, be mentioned as indicating that there is a sphere in which the extension of the functions of the State may be inevitable, in which, however, there lurk serious dangers. While there are some educationists who maintain that in the present division of conviction in religion, the education provided by the State must be entirely secular, and that in matters of faith the State must preserve neutrality; yet most of them agree that if religion be a necessary interest and activity of complete human personality, no education as the means of developing all the capacities would be effective which attempted to exclude so essential and crucial an element, for not only would one subject be omitted, but the presentation of other subjects would be injuriously affected. Instruction in the Bible is not sufficient for religious education: there must be a religious influence exercised on the scholars by the teachers not only in teaching this, but other subjects also. Theology must not supplant history and science, taught in the most approved methods; but the teacher's attitude to the world and life, religious or irreligious, will insensibly affect the quality and the effect of the teaching. The use of the school for sectarian teaching has led to lamentable controversies which have divided the Churches where a harmonious co-operation with the State would be of most value. There is an improvement, however, and efforts to reach common ground are being made. Despite all differences of the Churches, there is a large measure of agreement in Christian faith and duty, and that, if competently imparted, should be accepted as the maximum to be required in schools provided by the State for all the children of the nation. The questions of conscience which arise, will be dealt with in Chapter VII.

(*b*) While in the sphere of the conquest of Nature, especially the economic sphere—an increasing intervention of the State seems for the common good not only inevitable, but even desirable; and while in the regulation of social relations, except the most intimate personal, the State must have a voice; yet in the sphere of personal culture, using the word in the wide sense already defined, individual liberty and responsibility must be recognised.

Education must not be used by the State as it is being used in Italy, Germany, Russia and elsewhere, to mould the young mind into the shape which the immediate policy of the State desires. The State as expressing and giving effect to public opinion and popular sentiment, when it is democratic, or the ideas and purposes of the group or the person who controls it when it is autocratic, will always fall below the standard of the wisest and best minds. The largest measure of freedom, consistent with the purpose of education, the development of human personality, should be allowed to education authorities and teachers themselves. The cultural interests—art, literature, science, history, philosophy—should receive encouragement from the State in libraries, laboratories, museums, art-galleries, etc., but should be left free, so that gifted and competent persons can pursue their objects unhindered and unhampered in their own initiative, and under their own direction, or in voluntary association with others like-minded.

(c) There is a large sphere of conduct which necessarily falls under the control of the State. There must be righteousness in personal relations; one man must not do wrong to the person, the property, the character, the reputation of another; there may be even obligations of mutual help which the State may claim to enforce. In the relations of husband and wife, parent and child, employer and employed, buyer and seller, teacher and taught, there are rights and duties, recognised and enforced by the law. No man can say he has a right to do as he pleases with his own, for, as no man is self-made, despite the popular phrase, so no man has anything he can call exclusively his own, for he owes more to society than he can claim from it. But in all the nobler virtues and the finer graces, the service and the sacrifice inspired by love, each man has a right, no less than a duty, to form his conduct and character according to his own conscience. Only when that conscience in its dictates falls below the generally accepted standards of morals is the State entitled to prevent any injury to the community which might result from its free expression in conduct and character. If conscience is in advance of the moral standards, and is led to refuse what the State acting on those standards may claim the right to demand, the State will be wise to tolerate. The passive resister and the conscientious objector, acting from no anti-social motive, but from loyalty to conscience, had a claim to much more consideration than was given them. In the sphere of religion, especially the personal relation to God, the

State is an invader and a usurper if it claims any authority. This will be the subject of extended treatment in a subsequent chapter, and is here mentioned only for completeness.

(d) If the functions of the State are being thus extended, and both necessarily and desirably so for the common good, it is evident how important are the convictions and the character of those who are the agents of the State. It may not be able as the organ of community to rise in its policy much above the common beliefs and aims, because it must have regard to public opinion and popular sentiment, but the influence of the wisest and best citizens should be exerted to keep it as far ahead as is possible without altogether losing touch with the nation. And the idealist must recognise that his ideal can be realised only gradually, and that each partial realisation is itself educative, and prepares for a less inadequate. The *doctrinaire* who follows abstract principles regardless of concrete conditions, and the *opportunist* who thinks only of the immediate occasion, and the use of it for his individual interests, are both a hindrance to the endeavour to get the State to do the utmost practicable for the highest principles. Here the Church must be counsellor and helper of the State.

(1) THE previous chapter has shown the necessity of the State to Society for its historical evolution, and the inevitableness of the extension of its functions as that evolution leads from " homogeneity to heterogeneity, by differentiation and integration," to borrow Spencer's terms. Although not inconsistent with the divine will, not opposed to the divine providence, the State may be regarded as falling within the world, sensible and temporal, and revealing the invisible and eternal God in the same measure only as the general revelation in Nature and history.

(a) The Church, on the other hand, belongs to that unique supreme revelation of God, which culminates in the Incarnation of God as man in Christ, the redemption and the reconciliation of man through Him, the illumination and sanctification of the redeemed and reconciled by the Holy Spirit of God. It has its place in history, for " the Word became flesh," and tabernacled among men (John i. 14), but it is also *supra* as well as *intra-historical*. It issues

from the nature, character and purpose of God
with more immediate evidence of its divine
origin than Nature and history. While it toils
and suffers amid the earthlies, as did Christ,
yet it also reigns in Christ in the heavenlies
(Eph. i. 20–23). Hence is this chapter headed
the Mission of the Church, for as the Father
sent the Son to be the Saviour and the Lord
of mankind, so hath He sent His Church (John
xvii. 18), His body vitalised and invigorated
by His Spirit, into the world to be His complement in His completing of the divine purpose
that God shall be all things in all men (Eph. i. 23).
It is only such a vision of the Church as the
eternal purpose being fulfilled in time, as the
continuation of the Incarnation, as the habitation of God's Spirit, that can inspire the divided,
discouraged and distressed Christian community
on earth, as it must appear to the world, to
challenge with confidence and courage, un-
daunted and unafraid, the Anti-Christ of to-day
(II Thess. ii. 7), the secularism, the spirit of
the world without God, which is claiming the
throne of humanity, whether as Communism,
Fascism, Bolshevism, or National-Socialism. Only
a Church which knows itself to be of God and
for God alone can sustain the crusade against
all the forces of worldliness, wickedness, and
godlessness.

(*b*) It may seem to some that such a conception of the Church seems strange as expressed by a Protestant, Nonconformist, Congregationalist, who still accepts these names as defining his convictions within the earthly history of the Church as nearly as such terms can. But I hold my Protestantism, Nonconformity, Congregationalism subject to what I shall try to show is a transforming reservation. I believe in the divine objectivity, the œcumenical unity, the historical continuity of the Church as my inmost conviction in my personal relation to God, to which all these more outward convictions are subordinate. These are historically conditioned by a perversion in ecclesiastical faith and order. Because of this essential conviction, I believe that Protestantism reaffirmed the Gospel against Roman error; Nonconformity asserted that the Church can own no authority but Christ's; and Congregationalism gives expression in its organisation to the truth that the Presence of Christ and the Guidance of His Spirit in believers are sufficient for the worship, witness and work of His Church in any place at any time. But each of these lesser convictions is a partial application of that greatest conviction. Against a tendency to *subjectivism*, I must affirm that it is not the will of men, even believing men, to gather together for worship, witness and work that constitutes the Church. The Church is already present, as Christ is in the world, and that Presence is made manifest in the preaching of the Gospel, and in the administration of the sacraments as the signs and seals of the grace offered to faith in the Gospel. Against a tendency to sectarianism I must affirm that there is, and can be, only one Church, that the churches imperfectly express its content, and that only in their union will it be made adequately manifest. Against individualism I must affirm that a man must not exalt his own ideas and ideals as even for himself final; he must recognise that there is likely to be a wider knowledge, and a higher wisdom in the Christian community of all lands and all ages, and he must be prepared, not in servile subjection, but in grateful obedience to learn " the mind of Christ " in " the communion of the saints." A local congregation is *a church* only as in it and by it the one Church becomes manifest and active locally.

(*c*) Jesus proclaimed at the beginning of His ministry that the Kingdom of God is at hand (Mark i. 15), but at a later stage that the Kingdom of God " is in the midst of you " (Luke xvii. 21, R.V. margin). At first He openly proclaimed the nature of the Kingdom, the obligations it

imposed, the privileges it offered and the influence
it would exert as in the Sermon on the Mount
(Matt. v.–vii), where Matthew has collected sayings from different occasions, has modified them, as
a comparison with Luke shows, and has arranged
them in a manifesto of the Kingdom. At a
later stage, when, as the parable of the Sower
shows, He had discovered that only a small
number could or would receive the seed of
the Kingdom fruitfully, the Kingdom was presented in parables (Matt. xiii.) as a mystery
(a revelation that needed to be concealed in
symbols because the multitudes were not ready
for it, and it could be disclosed only to the few
discerning disciples). What was the Kingdom?
It was neither the *realm* of God in an ideal
human society, although that would be its
product, nor only a future *reign* of God, although
that would be a phase of it; it was the constant
rule of God, now made more manifest than in
times past, in Jesus Himself as the Messiah, but
to be made fully manifest only when He as
Messiah returned in power and glory. The
ethical and the eschatological aspects must
both be based upon the theological—God's
sovereignty. As Jesus' conception of His Messiah-
ship excluded both the popular expectations
and even the prophetic predictions of an earthly
deliverance and government, and included on

G

the one hand the content of the prophetic picture of the Suffering Servant (Isa. liii.), and on the other the apocalyptic vision of the Son of Man (Dan. vii. 13), the divine sovereignty manifest in Him, present and future, was a *saving sovereignty* (the theology being more distinctly defined in a soteriology).

(*d*) The current emphasis in English theology on the Kingdom as *realm*, an ideal human society brought about largely by human endeavour with some divine assistance, is, I am quite convinced, exegetically and still more theologically wrong; it represents the less adequate moral, and not the more adequate religious, standpoint, since the one lays stress on what man ought to do, and the other on what God does. An Anglican theologian has stated that the theology of the Church of England generally was Pelagian; and that is largely true of the Free Churches also, although Arminian might be a more accurate description. As I have elsewhere shown neither Augustinianism nor Calvinism is the necessary alternative; for there is a synthesis of the truth in each of these antitheses in a truer conception of the relation of God to man than any in which God's sovereignty and man's liberty are contrasted. As saving sovereignty it is not divine omnipotence suppressing human impotence, but divine grace evoking and sustaining human faith; there is a submission which is emancipation and a service which is freedom.[1] The Kingdom is neither an ideal to be realised, nor a consummation to be expected, although both are included in it; it is a present objective reality—God active with all His resources as God under human conditions redeeming men from sin and reconciling them unto Himself as His children. It is the Fatherhood at work in the Saviourhood and Lordship of Christ and the inner activity of the Spirit of God. The contrast made between the Church and the Kingdom as societies of narrower and wider scope is a false one. There are influences of the Kingdom which reach beyond any ecclesiastical boundaries or ecclesiastical agencies; but we conceive the Church inadequately if we think of it as primarily an ecclesiastical organisation; it is primarily a community of the Spirit of God, consisting of persons who, saved by grace, possess the Spirit in common. God's sovereignty in saving finds visible manifestation in time and space, inspiration energises in the world in organisation; but what is original, essential and central is the supreme activity of God, which is directly creative of the community of the Spirit, and

[1] See my book *Revelation through History and Experience*, pp. 162–164.

through human agency of the ecclesiastical organisation, to which, as human, attach imperfections which do not derive from the divine activity. We can conceive the Church aright only in such relation to the Kingdom of God.

(2) In expounding that conception in detail I am indebted to discussions in Germany on the nature of the Church for two suggestive distinctions. The Church is first the *object* of the Kingdom and then its *organ*. As organ it has its *soteriological* and its *sociological* aspect.

(*a*) As has already been indicated, God's supreme activity in Christ is "to save men to the uttermost," not as individuals only, but as social personality—that is, as members of a society. The parables in Luke xv. are often cited as the charter of the value of the human soul, and rightly so; but sometimes also in support of a religious individualism, and that wrongly; for the lost sheep is brought back to the flock, the last coin is replaced among the other coins, the son returns to the home. Jesus saved individuals, but He called His disciples into a community, and the founding of His Church was His aim. Evangelicalism has given quite a false emphasis in laying all the stress, as it sometimes has done, on future rewards and punishments for the individual souls, and has so encouraging an indifference to the fellowship in the Church, on which growth in grace depends, and to the claim of the world around, not for individual salvation only, but for a transformation of human society, so that God's will may be done on earth as it is in heaven. The religion of the Old Testament was not concerned about individual future destiny, but about the future destiny of the nation. The religion of the New Testament also moves within a community, and awaits a consummation for that community. Belief in individual personal immortality is a necessary and valuable part of the Christian faith; but it should not have the priority in the purpose of God for man. It is a redeemed and reconciled race that God as Father of all mankind wills. Ritschl puts the truth in a way determined by Lutheran dogmatics, when he says that the Church is the subject of justification by faith. Let me put it more broadly; it is the Church as the community of believers in the Spirit which is the *object* of the Kingdom of God, God's saving sovereignty. Men are saved, not for safety, but for service, or rather their safety lies in their service. They can freely receive only as they freely give (Matt. x. 8). Moral or religious selfishness is self-destruction of human personality. Hence the Church can be the *object* only as it becomes

the *organ* of the Kingdom. It is sometimes
foolishly said that God could save the world
without us Christians, but none has yet shown
how, for, as has been said before, God does
not rule by power, but by grace, and God's
grace in man keeps its divine quality of com-
municativeness. For us imperfect men there
may seem to be alternative ways, for divine
perfection there can be only one way—the
best; and what God has chosen is the only
way—the best. He who gives himself to service
knows that God is thus most surely and fully
saving him. Much of the inconsistency of Christian character is due to inadequate consecration
to the service of the Kingdom; much of the
loss of vitality and vigour in churches is due
to their being mutual benefit societies, and
not missionary, evangelisation agencies, a
heavenly leaven transforming the meal of earthly
society. This method of God in using saved
men for saving is in accord with His whole
creative method, where each stage of the created
is the condition of His further creating. Such
is the mutual dependence of the Church as
object and as organ of the Kingdom of God.

(*b*) This is the *soteriological* aspect of the
Church; it is the object and the organ of God's
saving sovereignty. Before passing to the
sociological it is desirable to develop more fully

what are the functions of the Church as the organ of the Kingdom. It seems to me that four of the figurative sayings of Jesus are rich in suggestion, two spoken directly to His disciples, two unfolding the mystery of the Kingdom. The disciples are the light of the world, the salt of the earth (Matt. v. 13–16), the Kingdom is like the mustard seed and the leaven (xiii. 31–33). I do not profess to be giving the historical exegesis, but a theological interpretation that the words allow.

(i) In I John it is said that " God is light, and in Him is no darkness at all " (i. 5). The Fourth Gospel represents Jesus as saying: " I am the Light of the World " (viii. 12). In Matthew Jesus bids His disciples: " Let your light so shine before men, that they may see your good works, and glorify your Father which is in heaven " (v. 16). Light is the physical symbol of personal perfection, the holy God, and Jesus has revealed that the holy God is the heavenly Father; and the disciples, in their lives as children of God, are to diffuse that revelation. The Christian Church does not in word and deed, in testimony and influence, in creed and character, declare truth discovered by human research, or grace achieved by human effort, but the divine revelation, which is also for sinful men redemptive and reconciling.

As interpreting the scriptures the historical record of revelation, under the guidance of the Spirit, it can echo the prophetic declaration: "Thus saith the Lord," the Master's voice: "I say unto you," and the apostolic pleading: "We are ambassadors therefore on behalf of Christ, as though God were intreating by us: we beseech you on behalf of Christ, be ye reconciled to God" (II Cor. v. 20). Its authority is not of man, but of God; but, as has been urged in the preceding paragraph, it is only as it continues the object that it can remain the organ of God's Kingdom. It is only as the presence of Christ, the operation of His Spirit is recognised in the preaching of the Gospel that it can prove to be "the power and the wisdom of God unto salvation" (Rom. i. 16; I Cor. i. 24). It is only as in the sacraments faith receives and responds to grace that they can be both signs and seals of the Gospel. Doubtless the Church has lost much of its authority, because it has failed to convince the world that it is the organ of God's sovereignty in truth and grace. Too many spheres of human interest and activity have asserted their autonomy or have been claimed by the State as its exclusive dominion because the Church has failed to interpret its Gospel in relation to "the whole manhood of all mankind," and to apply its principles to economics and politics and international relations. God's revelation is wide enough to cover the whole range of human thought and life; and the Church has not asserted its inclusiveness. Still more has the Church failed to make its light shine in "good deeds." Just as the seer is needed to apprehend the vision of God, so is the saint needed to translate that vision into actuality in human experience and character. The crisis is the judgment of God not only on the world for forsaking His way, but on the Church also for not in its "good deeds" making manifest His Word, the revelation of His Fatherhood in Christ.

(ii) This consideration leads us at once to the saying of Jesus about the salt. It is the savour of the salt on which He insists, not on any preserving or purifying quality it possesses. It is the distinctiveness of Christian experience and character that He here asserts, and He warns of the danger of that distinctiveness being lost, and of the world's loss also. "But if the salt have lost its savour, wherewith shall it be salted" (Mat. v. 13). The Church is always in danger of being conformed to the world, instead of being constantly transformed by the renewing of its mind (Rom. xii. 2). Adaptation to the historical environment for effective action is necessary, but compromise and accommodation are perilous. In adapting its theology to Greek philosophy, its polity to Roman imperialism, its ethics to the industrialism of to-day, it has not escaped the danger. The voice of the Church does not impress the world with its authority, because it often is little else or more than an echo of its clamours. This challenge of the totalitarian State is a summons that it should become a " totalitarian " Church, completely sanctified in its distinctiveness, so that through it the whole life of man may be purified and submitted unto God.

(iii) The Church as making its light shine, and preserving its savour, will be the agent of the expansion of the Kingdom of God as the small mustard seed becomes the great mustard plant. In the parable Jesus states this expansion as a fact and that fact has had confirmation in history. The small company of disciples has become the great multitude in many lands and many ages whom God has saved. But the expansion is no spontaneous evolution; the expansion of the Kingdom is the task of the Church. It must so bear its testimony and preserve its character, that men will be won for the Kingdom. The Church must be evangelising and missionary. Its self-preservation demands its self-propagation. Is not the danger to the

Church from any State due to the fact that most of the nations in Christendom are only nominally Christian, and that, even when the Christian profession is made, the heart is still pagan? The "German-Faith" movement of which more will need be said later, is a neo-paganism; and even in Great Britain government often falls so short of Christian standards, because masses have lapsed from Christian belief and morals. Unevangelised Asia and Africa may challenge even more dangerously than any movements in Europe the dominance of the Christian faith.

(iv) The parable of the leaven is a complement to the parable of the mustard seed; and in some measure relieves the anxiety which has just been expressed. The influence of Christianity spreads beyond the confines of the Church, and is secretly present, active and transforming in society. Many a Hindu, who on patriotic and domestic grounds refuses to confess Christ, is in his standard of conduct Christian; so also in other lands not yet fully evangelised. The modern forms of ancient faiths—Neo-Hinduism, Neo-Buddhism, Neo-Islam—bear witness to this influence. We must not, however, be too confident as to its potency, for there are many counteracting influences. In the foreign mission-field secularism has become a more formidable foe than the native religions; and it is with European culture and civilisation that this secularism has spread. In this hindrance to its foreign missions the Church is paying the penalty for leaving so many in the home lands unevangelised, and for allowing so many professing Christians to lose their distinctiveness, to fall so far below the Christian standards in so many of their activities, cultural, economic and political. Thus from overseas comes the confirmation of the summons, that it is only as the Church is not *of* this world that it can *in* the world effectively discharge its functions as the human agency for the divine activity in saving men.

(*c*) By the *sociological* aspect of the Church we mean the Church as an association of men, whose community lies in their common new life by the Spirit of God, for work, witness and worship through the institutions of the preaching of the Gospel, and the administration of the sacraments (the common Protestant conception), and the exercise of discipline (the addition in the Reformed Church). The first important question in this connection is what is the relation of the sociological to the soteriological aspect:

(i) One view is that there is a necessary connection between faith and order, between the function and the structure of the Church. As

God has appointed the function, so He has provided the structure. To preserve the unity and the continuity of the Church against heresy (false doctrine) and schism (wrong division) God has willed the apostolic succession in the historic episcopate for the valid ordination of the ministry and the valid administration of sacraments. This is what is called the " Catholic " view, and it prevails in Roman, Greek, and Anglo-Catholicism. The Church of England is not committed to this view by its creed or polity, but it is, if not the prevalent, yet the most articulate and so dominant view.

(ii) Another view is that, since the New Testament does not prescribe any particular organisation, and since the organisation which was developed in the first three centuries was an adaptation to the temporary conditions, and was affected by the local environment, it cannot be held that only one type of polity can claim divine approval and authority; and therefore under the guidance of God's Spirit the organisation may now, as in the early centuries, assume the form which, under the changed conditions, will make it most effective for the discharge of this function. This is the modern Protestant view, and is held by Episcopalians, Presbyterians and Congregationalists, although the adherents of each of these types have an

inherited or acquired preference for it. The
Protestant sects at their beginning did, however, make a more exclusive claim. Calvinism
favoured the conciliar type, and claimed a divine
right for Presbyterianism; the early Separatists
believed that they were reforming the Church
according to the New Testament, without
" tarrying for any "—queen or bishop. The
lessons of history cannot be disregarded. We
have in the New Testament the germs of later
developments (I Cor. xii. 28). The apostles
held a distinctive personal authority because of
their intimate relations to Christ; the prophets,
evangelists, teachers were variously endowed
by the Spirit and were an itinerant ministry of
evangelisation and edification; the local administration of the churches was by the pres-
byters or overseers (bishops) and the deacons.
In the development of the Church there have
emerged the three types mentioned—episcopacy,
presbytery and congregation. And in the conversations between Anglicans and Free Church-
men at Lambeth it has been agreed that the
three types should be preserved, and there has
just been offered to the churches for their consideration a sketch of what a united Church—
episcopal, presbyteral and congregational—might
be. Adaptations there should be to make the
churches as effective for their functions as can

be; in the foreign field among the younger churches this European development should not be regarded as normative, but the genius of each people or race should be allowed expression. It is probable, however, that for some generations at least these younger churches will follow the older churches which brought them the Gospel.

(iii) A third view, not spontaneously arising within the churches, but rather imposed by historical conditions, concedes to the State the determination of the organisation of the Church. In the Hebrew nation, as in all the nations in antiquity, Church and State were inseparable; an Israelite believed and worshipped Yahveh. After the Exile Judaism was a Church, but depended for any freedom it enjoyed in religion on the arbitrary will of the ruler. The Christian Church was not linked to the life of a nation, although it claimed, by its acceptance of Jesus as the Christ, to be the true Israel, as the use of the word *ecclesia* shows. Sometimes tolerated, sometimes persecuted by the Roman Empire, its organisation was influenced by that of the State. In the Middle Ages the Western Church and the Holy Roman Empire were the two complementary aspects of Christendom, although even before the Reformation the independent nations resented and resisted the encroachments of Rome. John Wyclif was the protagonist of England against Rome. At the Reformation it was assumed, with the exception of some sects, that the State had not only a right, but a duty in regard to the right ordering of the Church. Calvinism asserted the Church's spiritual authority, but was prepared to use the State for the enforcement of its decrees. In view of the controversy which will engage our attention in a later chapter, it is interesting to consider Luther's view, although there has been dispute about it, but I follow Troeltsch in my brief statement.[1] As a spiritual reality—that is, in its *soteriological* aspect—the Church is of God's appointment, not man's choice. Wherever the Gospel is truly preached and the sacraments are duly administered according to God's ordinance there is the Church. He believed that the Roman Church had forfeited its claim, and that, relying on the authority of the Scriptures, he in his conception of the Gospel was restoring the Church. At first, it would seem, he believed that the Christian people, gathered together by faith in God's grace, would suffice for the ordering of the Church in its organisation; but the excesses of some of the fanatical sectaries

[1] *The Social Teaching of the Christian Churches*, English Translation, II, pp. 515–521.

and the Peasants' Wars aroused his native conservatism; and he " put his trust in princes." *Cujus regio, ejus religio* was the formula in which this dependence of Church on State was expressed. Lutheranism in other countries retained its bishops, but in Germany they gave place to superintendents, through whom the ruler kept his guiding hand on the Church. It must be remembered that till the Revolution of 1918 the Lutheran and the Reformed churches were thus in subjection to rulers. The " German Christians," of whom we shall afterwards have much to say, are not innovators, but are reviving an old tradition. The Opposition are striving to maintain the new-found freedom since 1918.

(*d*) For our present purpose it is necessary to call attention to a distinction on which Troeltsch lays great stress, that between the church and the sect type.[1] The church is a historical entity, it has had a continuous history; there are certain marks which distinguish it from any other human association, and attest its objectivity as not of man but of God. These have already been mentioned. Wherever and whenever the Gospel is truly preached, the sacraments are duly administered, and the Reformed added discipline is enforced, there the

[1] *Op. cit.*, pp. 691–694.

H

Church is. Those who in any nation have been
baptised, and do not expressly repudiate their
connection and refuse its ordinances as at
confirmation, marriage, and burial constitute
its membership. It is the *Volkskirche*, the people's
Church, and all within its territorial limits have
a claim on its ministrations. Those who welcomed the measure of freedom from the State
gained at the Revolution, and the Confessional
Opposition now desire to maintain this character.
In view of this historical continuity, and the
objectivity of its ordinances it claims to be the
Church, which preserves the true confession,
and so has the lawful authority. The sect,
on the other hand, has separated itself from
the Church because it condemns its errors
and wrongs, and seeks to bear a witness of its
own to divine truth and grace; it disregards
unity and continuity, and bases its claim to
be a Church, or even the Church, on the personal experience and character of its members
as converted men, who must come out from
among the unconverted adherents of the Church,
and must reform the community thus gathered
without regard for or even in defiance of the
existing ecclesiastical authority. As has been
indicated, Luther leaned towards the sect-type
when he looked to the Christian people for
the ordering of the Church. Calvinism, in

its emphasis on discipline, inclines to the sect-type, inasmuch as it attaches importance to the personal experience and character of its members. The Church type claims objectivity in the continuity of its external ordinances, in which the divine truth and grace are presented to men for their acceptance and blames the sect-type for its subjectivity in basing the Church on human faith, the experience and the character of the members. Lutheranism appeals against Calvinism in regard to the secondary place it gives to discipline to the parable of the wheat and the tares (Matt. xiii. 24–30). The Church tolerates them side by side, as the Lord commanded: the sect roots up the tares, and some of the wheat also. I am freely paraphrasing; but I am, I believe, giving an accurate impression. Our Free Churches would fall into the sect rather than the Church type; German Lutheranism as a whole distrusts the idea of a free Church, and adheres to the people's Church. From what has been said already, it will be clear that my convictions, and not mere inclinations, lead me to the sect-type. The Church can make the light shine only as the salt keeps its savour. One German writer feels this enough to propose that within the people's Church, the truly Christian in life as well as belief should form around the pastor an inner group, the centre of its wider testimony and influence. But at the same time I repudiate sectarianism, censoriousness and exclusiveness, and seek to preserve the basis of the Church as the organ of God's saving activity in the world in its unity and continuity, in its objectivity in presenting in its Gospel and sacraments the truth and grace of God in Christ.

(e) Luther's emphasis on the corporeal presence of Christ *in*, *with*, and *under* the elements (consubstantiation) was not merely sacramentalism, for he always subordinated the sacraments to the Gospel, but was zeal for the Gospel of the real saving presence of Christ—the objectivity of grace, whether faith responded to it or not; always available, whether accepted or not. To a subjective individualism, which lays such stress on the receptivity and responsiveness of faith as to give the impression that the human condition is creative of the divine reality, instead of recognising that it is the divine reality of grace which evokes the human faith, this teaching is a salutary correction; what is to be regretted is that Luther bound up the truth of Christ's presence in the sacraments with an artificial metaphysics. While the Catholic type of Christianity will tend to this " church " conception, and the Protestant to the " sect " conception, the two do not necessarily go together.

A man may be a Nonconformist towards the "Catholic" polity, and yet not inclined to the sect extreme of exalting the authority of the individual preferences above the authority which the Church in its unity and continuity as an objective reality in history possesses. In view of the special interest in this volume, it must be here added, that the authority of the State cannot be so confidently challenged by individual or denominational interpretations or applications of Christianity as by a *consensus* of the Christian churches, making manifest that unity and continuity of the Church not in its *sociological* aspect as a human organisation, but in its *soteriological* aspect as a divine agent; and it is one of the tragedies of history that the differences about the human organisation have so often hindered and enfeebled the Church's testimony and influence as divine agent for the salvation of mankind.

(1) THERE is no essential antagonism between Church and State, as of grace
and sin, liberty and law, God and man,
for, as has been argued, the State has not been
appointed by God solely or mainly for the
restraint of sin by force, and the Church is not
in the world to destroy, but to fulfil law in
liberty. How they may work harmoniously for
the good of society will be shown in the next
chapter; here we must not only glance at such
conflicts as have occurred in the past, but give
a closer scrutiny to the acute controversies of
the present time.

(a) In the Hebrew nation not only were
priests and prophets at strife with one another,
but the Kings refused the prophets' guidance.
The story of Jeremiah is a moving instance of
suffering for witness to God's word. The sacrifice and heroism of the Maccabees can be
placed alongside of the fidelity unto death of
the Covenanters of a later age. The martyr-
doms of the Roman Empire have their modern
parallels in China and Russia. The Empire

and the Papacy in the Middle Ages were in theory complementary, both necessary for Christendom; but in practice they were often at variance. Kings of England were often engaged in controversy with the Pope. The persecutions of the Reformation period were inflicted not solely by the State on the Church, but within the Church divided against itself. In all these conflicts it cannot be claimed that the State was always wrong and the Church always right. While churches, when persecuted, asserted their claim to religious liberty, yet, when clothed with power, they forgot that plea. It must be confessed that while the divisions of Christendom after the Reformation made mutual toleration a practical necessity, it was not the churches who were foremost in asserting the theoretical principle. In State establishments of the Church there is an acceptance of dependence on, and control by, the State which seems altogether inconsistent with the " Crown rights of the Redeemer." It is probable that in the Church of England the yoke of the State is less galling than it has ever been elsewhere; but even here the Church had to submit to the humiliation of being refused the right in law of using the Revised Prayer-Book, a humiliation which, in my judgment, has not been annulled by the tolerance of its illegal use with the approval of the bishops. As a Nonconformist, I recognise the injustice which the State inflicts on other churches by the privileges which it accords to one Church, although for me the disadvantages of such a connection with the State seem to outweigh the privileges. As one who loves the Church of England as a Church, I should like to see that Church itself claim its emancipation, even if it meant sacrifice. Outside of England there are in the British Commonwealth no established churches, also in the United States of America. But even in these favoured lands there are requirements of the State which the Christian conscience refuses, and to which reference will be made in a later chapter. On the Continent the State is suspicious of the Church; and, even where there is no endowment, seeks to impose on the Church a legal status, which aims at averting the assumed dangers of its independent action. With the Roman Catholic Church there are Concordats, which endeavour to reconcile the rival claims to supreme authority. The Free Churches in the Continental countries are not as free as our British churches are. My own conviction is that, not only to obey God alone, but even to render the best service it can to the State itself, the Church must be entirely independent of the State, not waiting on its smile, nor dreading its frown.

(*b*) Neutrality there cannot be, hostility there need not be, co-operation there ought to be if the State is to discharge its functions most efficiently, and if the Church is to fulfil its mission faithfully. For let it be clearly understood, a slogan such as " A free Church in a free State," does not correspond to the actual situation; since Church and State are not separate departments of society closed the one to the other. The extension of the functions of the State, necessary and desirable as it has been shown to be, to include almost (if not quite), the whole range of human life, and the wider vision by the Church of its mission to save from sin for God; " the whole manhood of all mankind " make their spheres nearly coterminous. Motive, method and means may be different, but the sphere of service is the same, the whole man, not the body as the charge of the State, and the soul as the care of the Church.

(*c*) There would have been a problem of adjustment even if the political development had been normal, *i.e.* government of the people by the people for the people as its goal; but as a result of the War and the avoidable and perverse consequences of the War, reaction has generally prevailed, democracy has been discredited, dictatorship has triumphed, and the State has become more arrogant and in-

tolerant in its claims. The theory of the " totalitarian " State has been formulated to justify the
practice of ambitious and fanatical claimants
of power. The Peace treaties, instead of allevi-
ating the evils resulting from the War, aggra-
vated them, for vengeance was their motive,
and not magnanimity. Despite the provision
for a League of Nations to preserve peace and
prevent war, an endeavour to give internationalism an effective agent, nationalism has become
more extreme, inflamed by ambition or resentment. The pre-war enmities were stimulated
and not suppressed. The hope of economic
recovery in the early post-war years soon faded
like a vain dream; and an economic nationalism
has brought unemployment, distress, discontent,
so that the present situation can without exaggeration be described as a world-crisis, of which
the issue—ruin or recovery—is still uncertain.
Governments have not only failed to lessen,
but by mistaken policies have increased the evils.
Democracy through its organ, parliamentary
government, has seemingly proved a failure.
The hasty assumption is not justified that democracy is inherently bad; all the facts show is
that democracy has shared the imperfections of
man; instead of regard for the common good
as the real, and not only the pretended motive
of political action there have been partisanship,

rivalries, intrigues, ambitions polluting the stream of public opinion and popular sentiment; there have been imperfect knowledge, unsound judgment, too narrow a vision. The peoples were crying out, "Who will show us any good?" Exasperated and despairing, they were ready to acquiesce in, if not to approve of, any form of government that promised to remove their miseries, satisfy their wants and revive their hopes. We must recognise that the success, such as it is, of the dictatorships is largely due to this morbid state of mind. Resistance to the violence there would have been had there still been faith in the existing modes of government.

(*d*) What appeared as the need of the hour was *strong* government—government not weakened by differences, discords, divisions, but strong in unity, controlling all the resources of the nation to make it secure, prosperous and contented at home and respected abroad. Such unity seemed to be best obtained by the absolute dominance of a group, agreed on its policy, or what would be even more effective, a group, devoted to, and directed by *one* leader. The permanent and general tendency to hero-worship, to devotion and loyalty to a person rather than a principle or institution, determined the direction in which in their desperate need the peoples looked for effective deliverance. In so wide-spread a phenomenon as this of dictatorship supplanting democracy external conditions do not exclusively determine events; there must be inward desires, motives, impulses. The practice came before the doctrine, and the establishment of dictatorships has led to the exposition of the totalitarian state. As the name clearly indicates, what is meant by the totalitarian state is that the State claims to have the direction and control of the *total* interests and activities of the community. If thought remains free, its expression can be controlled. Science, art, philosophy, history, education, morals, and even religion fall under the authority of the State. It is true that the State may not assert that authority, that it may for its own ends exempt parts of that total from its direct control; but the right is claimed, as on occasion the power is used, to bring into subjection interests and activities which have been allowed some independence. The State is, if not *de facto*, yet *de jure* (as it interprets its *jus*) *total* director and controller of the whole nation.

(*e*) The Duce Mussolini may in Italy come to an agreement with the Papacy which seems to concede more to the Vatican than any previous government had done, and he may also concede toleration to the Protestant sects; but, as his words show, that involves no recognition of any independent authority of the Church alongside of that of the State, but it is in the interests of the State meanwhile to avoid any quarrel. In the last resort the State remains supreme. The Fascist formula is: "Nothing against the State; nothing outside the State; everything for the State." In Russia a group is carrying through an economic revolution in a ruthless fashion, sacrificing human lives without any consideration to insure its success, respecting no personal rights where these would be a hindrance, seizing grain for export while the peasants, especially those who still till their own soil, are dying of starvation, and even putting hindrances in the way of relief. It is pretended that religious worship is tolerated; but while this is to some extent true, the churches are deprived of their treasures in icons, altars, bells; churches are being seized and put to other uses; a cathedral becomes an Anti-God museum; ministers of religion (not orthodox priests alone) are under mere pretexts imprisoned or exiled; and do not get the food card on the ground that they are economically useless; and many are forced to earn their bread in some trade. The instruction of children in religion is forbidden, and the public schools are godless, children being taught to sneer at the superstition of their parents. An Anti-God propaganda is encouraged and supported, while religious propaganda is forbidden. Atheism is an essential element in the theory which is being applied in the total activities of the State. In Austria also a reactionary government under Roman Catholic influences, despite protestations of the equality of all religious confessions before the law, is inflicting through minor officials many hardships and injustices on the small Protestant minority. Although bound by a minority treaty to grant to the German Protestants transferred by the change of frontiers from German to the alien Polish rule—freedom of religion, use of their mother-tongue, education in that tongue and religion—the Government of Poland has oppressed its new subjects, and has even had the effrontery to repudiate the obligations which it had accepted. Among the Ruthenes, too, in Southern Poland, transferred from Austrian rule, there has been ill-treatment of Protestants. Baptist, Unitarian, Lutheran, and Reformed groups have been unjustly dealt with by the Rumanian authorities. Probably at no time for some centuries has the hand of the State pressed so heavily on religious minorities. These facts have been so briefly mentioned to correct a prevalent impression that it is only in Germany that there is such a conflict between Church and State. Although, through various channels of communication, some strictly confidential, I have been kept in close touch with what is going on in these other lands, I have more adequate and intimate knowledge of the situation in Germany. Besides this reason for restricting the discussion now to Germany the character of the conflict there has special interest and importance.

(2) Even as a boy, I followed with eager interest the unification of Italy and of Germany as victories for national liberty. The irony of history! These two nations are now subjected to tyranny and are accepting that subjection. In both this tyranny appears as the defence of liberty against the aggression of other nations. In Germany, as in Italy, the idea of unity dominates, and has been in Germany consistently worked out to its extreme consequences.

(a) While I detest and condemn the motives and methods of Anti-Semitism, yet I must admit that in most Continental countries the Jews are a menacing problem, an economic danger. Many of them are *in* a country to get all they can *out* of it, and not *of* that country to give what they can *to* it. In manners, habits and religion they are an alien element. Christendom, by the persecutions of the past, is largely responsible for having made them what they are. While there was Anti-Semitism in Germany before the War, yet that prejudice has become more general and acute because of the share of foreign Jews, who came in from the East, in bringing about economic ruin in the time of inflation, and fostering, as it is with some ground alleged, moral and political corruption. Such a charge lies only against a section of Jews. Many were quite at home in Germany, good citizens, and making more than their proportionate contribution to the civilisation and culture of the nation. For the general persecution of Jews, or persons of Jewish descent, the worst which could be said against them affords no excuse and it is a " blot on the scutcheon " of a great nation which will remain. This prejudice afforded the occasion or provocation to give actuality to an abstract theory of *race*. In the New Germany there must be one nation, the Germanic, the Nordic, the Aryan, terms of narrower and wider compass at the advocate's pleasure. The German people, if less mixed in blood than the British, is not pure; as many a name shows there is a large Slavonic infusion, and yet this fiction of *one* pure-blooded German nation is one article of the creed of National-Socialism, and is used to exclude Jews from public offices, professions, etc.

(*b*) The unification of Germany did not mean one State, but rather a federation of states, under the domination of Prussia, the King of which became German Emperor. Kingdoms, princedoms, dukedoms, etc., survived in large numbers with a considerable measure of self-governments. What Bismarck did not venture to do, that National-Socialism undertook, *i.e.* to bring all these states into one State, and has succeeded in doing. A unification of the Government has been carried through, and for the present at least appears likely to remain. The National-Socialist Party has also the wider ambition to include Austria, and even, although the intention is less openly disclosed, the German-speaking parts of Czecho-Slovakia in the one German nation and State.

(*c*) Within this unity only one policy—that of the Nazis—is to be tolerated; unanimity is secured by the suppression of all contrary opinions. Concentration camps are an effective method of persuasion, and even violence was resorted to in the earlier stages, but has been discouraged in the later. Control of the press, the wireless, the picture-house gives the party in power a monopoly in influence on public opinion, although there appears now to be more toleration for the expression of unauthorised views. A German visitor told me that very

I

few people in Germany knew what was going on unless they read foreign papers, as he did, and on occasion the sale of these papers is prohibited. A speech which I made on the struggle within the Church was reported in one of our papers, and the circulation of that number was stopped. Within the party which thus seeks to impose its policy differences of opinion sometimes emerge; even rival ministers take opposing action. But a more or less drastic purge from time to time restores the party to the appearance of agreement.

(d) This idea of unity—nation, state, policy— is incarnated in the person of the one leader, Herr Adolf Hitler, who was born an Austrian subject, but by his eloquence has gained an influence which it is given to few men to wield. Did he not embody the *Zeitgeist* it is probable that that gift would not have sufficed. It is not necessary for our purpose to pronounce any judgment on his capacity and character. He seems genuinely desirous of maintaining peace, for the present at least, and has in the Church controversy occasionally appeared as a moderating influence. While he is often spoken of in the most exaggerated language of adulation and devotion, and has gained a large measure of confidence among many persons who do not belong to the Nazi party, he is not in fact possessed of as absolute authority as he is invested with in theory, for there are many persons, of whose wishes and aims he must take account in shaping his policy, and there are sometimes voices heard which are not merely an echo of his. Whatever movements of opposition there are, they are underground, and have not yet been able to end " the brave show " of unity.

(3) Even although in Germany the influence of the Christian churches has been much less than in Great Britain and America, and although the working-classes, not only in the towns, but even in the country, were estranged from the Church, this purpose of unification could not exclude them.

(a) There were two reasons for the action taken, one more theoretical and one more practical. In the political ideal just described there runs the one guiding and dominating principle— *unity* demanding *uniformity*. The churches must be brought into that unity, and their organisation must be moulded into conformity with that of the nation (*Gleichschaltung*). As is the State, so must the Church be. The Church with such authority and influence as it possessed must be made an obedient tool of the State. No attempt was made to carry out this intention completely. About a third of Germany is Roman

Catholic, and that universal Church could not be fitted into any national ecclesiastical organisation. Possibly had there not been this insuperable obstacle, the incorporation of the Protestant churches into the State system would have gone further. As the independence of the Roman Catholic Church was recognised, and a Concordat was concluded, by which the Church as such was excluded from any political activity, the independence of the Protestant churches must be at least nominally recognised. The Free Churches—that is, those which have not had any connection with the State, and in principle refuse its support, such as the Methodists and the Baptists, have been left alone, although general legislation imposes some restrictions on their freedom of action. Probably this exemption is because their numbers are comparatively few, and because as the fruits of missionary enterprise from Great Britain and the United States, they might claim a support from their mother denominations which would involve complications abroad. The Churches with which we are concerned are the native churches of Germany, the Lutheran and the Reformed, whose beginnings go back to the Reformation.

(b) For that movement it was lamentable that it was weakened by division for which Luther's intolerant dogmatism was largely responsible. Because Zwingli, the Swiss Reformer, would not accept his too literal interpretation of the words of Christ: " This is my body " (Mark xiv. 22) on which he based his doctrine of consubstantiation or the corporeal presence of Christ *in*, *with*, and *under* the bread and the wine, he refused any further fellowship with him; and thus the German and the Swiss movements fell apart. Calvin was Zwingli's successor as the leader of the Swiss movement. Early Protestantism assumed two types—the Lutheran, sometimes called the Evangelical, and the Calvinistic, generally spoken of as Reformed. While in Germany the Lutheran type is the prevalent, yet the Reformed type is in some districts largely represented. As has been already indicated, Luther distrusted the Christian people as the directing and controlling agency in the Church, and relied on the authority of the princes favourable to the Reformation. The political circumstances in Germany led in the same direction, and the guiding principle was, *Cujus regio*, *ejus religio*—the ruler was to determine whether his territory was to remain Roman Catholic or become Protestant; but the Protestants in a Roman Catholic territory might migrate to a Protestant, and *vice versa*. Although movements of the population since have modified this territorial separation of the confession, yet to-day even the country is divided into districts, predominantly Catholic or Protestant. In the Protestant territories the Church became dependent on and controlled by the State. The idea of a Free Church is foreign and uncongenial to the German mind generally, and most of the Christians in Germany find nothing anomalous, as we Nonconformists in England and even a growing number of Anglicans do, in a subjection of the Church to the State. Each independent ruler controlled his own church, and in 1918 there were forty-one territorial churches, some Lutheran, some Reformed, and some in which by political action the Lutheran and the Reformed had been brought under one organisation, as in Prussia. Each citizen had to state some church affiliation, unless he had by a legal formality severed his connection with any, and a church-rate was levied by the State. When at the Revolution of 1918 these churches gained their independence, in some states the church-rate was still collected, but handed over to the ecclesiastical organisation, in others the churches were thrown back on their own resources. The number of territorial churches was reduced to twenty-eight, and a federation was formed for mutual counsel and support. It could not interfere in the internal administration of the territorial churches, but could arrange for concerted action in other matters. To give an instance: the Federation was represented officially at the Stockholm Life and Work Conference, 1925, but it did not appoint any delegates to the Lausanne Faith and Order Conference, 1927. Hence the " German Christian " party now dominating the new United Church claimed the right to appoint the representatives to the Universal Council, which is continuing the work of Stockholm, whereas it was only by courtesy that it was granted a place in the Continuation Committee of Faith and Order.

(c) This Federation prepared the minds of many for the unification of the churches in the German Evangelical Church, which was the first step taken in the path of conforming the organisation of the Church to that of the State, and this step was agreed to by the Committee of the Federation. The proposal that there should be as head of the Church, as Chancellor Hitler was head of the State, a *Reichsbishof*, with a number of provincial bishops under his authority, was also accepted, and indeed some of the territorial churches had after 1918 appointed bishops instead of General Superintendents. Dr. Arnold von Bodelschwingh was nominated by the provisional Committee framing the new constitution as *Reichsbishof*, and as he bore a highly honoured name and was worthy of it, this nomination found general acceptance, even among the Reformed Churches, which were opposed to Episcopacy as Lutheranism never has been. This, however, did not suit the aims of the " German Christian " party, who had the support of the Government, and its intervention in the dispute compelled the resignation of the *Reichsbishof*. By means not free from reproach, this party secured a majority in the synods, etc., and got their nominee, Müller, an army chaplain and confidant of the Chancellor, elected; and it became evident that, while the State professed neutrality he would have the support of the State in the measures he took to get his authority imposed. The personal objection to him was strengthened by the tolerance which he extended to extreme heretical views, and the majority of pastors, in most cases with the support of their congregations, joined the opposition, not because they objected to the unification of the Church or the episcopate, but because they were suspicious of the *Reichsbishof's* theological attitudes and feared that the Gospel and the Reformation Confessions which interpreted it were in danger of being displaced by a paganised nominal Christianity. The opposition does not primarily stand for the Church's independence of the States, for German Lutheranism, and even Calvinism, do not hold the conviction: "a free Church in a free State," but they are most of all contending for the preservation of the faith of the Reformation. They, with the "German Christians," still hold by the conception of a *Volkskirche*, a national Church, of which all citizens, unless they expressly exclude themselves, are assumed to be members, and to the ordinances of which they may lay claim, since for Luther the objectivity of the Church depended not primarily on the Christian experience and character of a voluntary membership, but on the true preaching of the Gospel and the right administration of the sacraments, which the ruler was expected to secure. In one book called *The Century of the Church* the liberation from State control was welcomed as beginning a new era for the Church; no longer a department of State it had entered on a century of opportunity to evangelise the nation. The revival of the spirit of the nation by the Hitler regime was welcomed by many, now in opposition, as a fresh opportunity to make the nation more than nominally Christian.

(*d*) So far there is some common ground between the opposition, now called the Confessional Church, and the "German Christians."

The orthodoxy of many of them there is no adequate ground to question, although the action of the *Reichsbishof* has aroused this suspicion and fear. But it is not uncharitable to say that some of this party are more zealous for the nation than for the Gospel. Assuming that the National-Socialist ideal represents the mind of the nation, they argue that the Church can recover the estranged masses, and be again the *Volkskirche* if it identifies itself openly with the Nazi policy, and conforms not in outward structure only, but in its purpose with the State as that now is. It is, however, an assumption which may before long be disproved that the estranged masses approve the policy of the Government, and will be reconciled to the Church if it accepts and promotes that policy. The contrary is much more probably the case. For this conforming to the dominant world-view Luther is appealed to, and his dualism accepted; the sphere of grace, in which men are justified by faith, is distinguished from the sphere of the civic order, in which the Christian believer must be prepared to submit to the powers that be. The measures which the *Reichsbishof* has employed on asserting his arbitrary rule, the deposition of pastors, the employment of police, etc., are also justified by an appeal to Luther. As Luther approved the use of force by the princes in securing the submission of their subjects, so may force be used in establishing the new church order which has the sanction of the State. The " German Christians " thus claim that they, and not their opponents, are in the historical succession to Luther; and there are passages in his writings in which he immoderately expresses himself which lend some countenance to their pleadings.

(e) A crucial instance of this apologetic is the casuistry by which the enforcement of the Aryan clause excluding Jews in the Church is defended. It is to the honour of the leading New Testament scholars of Germany that they issued a declaration against this clause as altogether inconsistent with the Gospel, and the theological faculty of the University of Marburg asserted the same conviction. While it was generally conceded that the exclusion of persons who were of Jewish descent, or were married to those of Jewish descent from the *membership* of the Christian churches would be contrary to the principle of Christian universalism, that in Christ there is neither Jew nor Gentile, Greek nor barbarian; yet one Old Testament scholar appealed to Hebrew Christians to show so much consideration for the Aryan Christians, who shared the general Anti-

Semitism, and to whom, therefore, their presence
was unwelcome, as to withdraw themselves, of
their own accord, and to form a separate Hebrew
Christian Church; and to this plea he added
the reason that only as a separate community
could they bear witness to Jesus as the Messiah,
whom their own people had rejected, and thus
fulfil their distinctive historical function. For
the application of this Aryan clause to the
ministry of the Church, the argument was advanced, that while the Church as the organ of
the saving grace of God must preserve its universalism, yet as a human society within the
nation, it should conform its practice to that
of the State, it should not go contrary to the
currents of popular sentiment, it should adapt
itself to the conditions of the time, as Paul did
in his instructions regarding women in Corinth.
We may marvel at the ingenuity, we may
even concede the sincerity of these arguments,
but we cannot admit their cogency.

(f) Even if we allow that the Left wing of
the German Christian party can still claim
to be in some sense Christian, yet there are
other movements clamouring for recognition
by the State as religions, which are a relapse,
in varied forms, into paganism, and are in more
or less degree opposed to Christianity, whether
Roman Catholic or Protestant. In some cases

Anti-Semitism is the motive of the rejection of Christianity because of its connection with the Old Testament. Paul is derided as Jewish. Where some respect for Jesus is retained, the suggestion is sometimes made, that as the population of Galilee was mixed, He was probably an Aryan, and not a Semite. In other cases it is the Christian Ethics of love, forgiveness and sacrifice which is the offence, as contrary to the heroic warlike Germanic spirit. Germany can never be strong in the assertion of its inherent greatness, so long as this pacifism and internationalism bring weakness. The nationalist mysticism—the nation or race as the object of adoration and devotion—bases itself sometimes on a pantheism in which a kinship with the Aryan religion of India is claimed. The German genius is one of the manifestations of the ultimate reality. This is the " German Faith " movement. National-Socialism claims to have saved Germany from Anti-God Bolshevism, and was for that reason welcomed and approved by many of the Christians of Germany. But in these varied movements, all inspired by an extreme nationalism, and all aiming to give a *rationale* for National-Socialism, there is a serious peril—a neo-paganism. For this arrogant and exclusive nationalism or racialism, and this exaltation of the State as the absolute authority over the thought and life of men is inherently anti-Christian, a challenge of the sole universal authority, the redemptive and reconciling sovereignty of the divine grace in Christ as Saviour and Lord.

(g) I have in the preceding sketch avoided bewildering the reader by any attempt to describe the ebb and the flow of the controversy as within the Church itself, or as affected by the wavering and inconsistent policy of the State, sometimes insisting on the neutrality of the State in an inter-Church dispute and some-times lending support to the " German Chris-tian " party and the *Reichsbishof*.[1] As this is being written a more active intervention of the State seems probable. It is evident that it is in the interests of national unity that the controversy should be ended; but mere sup-pression would not restore any real unity, and would weaken the loyalty of the suppressed section to " the Leader " himself. The German Government has discovered, as many a govern-ment has discovered before, that to challenge the Christian conscience is to enter on a struggle in which the apparent defeat of the Church has proved real victory, as on Calvary's Cross.

(4) I have endeavoured in what precedes

---

[1] See note at the end of the volume, p. 237.

to be as unprejudiced and as impartial as I could be. I have avoided mentioning names or giving references to books, as I have friends on both sides, and do not wish to forfeit the friendship even of those who in my judgment are most mistaken and wrong. For even in offering an account of this controversy, one is bound, so far as one has any influence, to continue " the ministry of reconciliation " which the relation of Germany to other nations to-day so insistently demands. In this conflict, wherever it may be waged—and it has been shown that it is being waged not in Germany alone— the Church must show that it has the authority superior to that of the State not only in so far as it is concerned with the supreme interest of human life—the realisation of the human ideals in man's relation to God—but inasmuch as in dependence on the guidance and the support of the Spirit of God, it is the interpreter and the agent of the purpose of God as not only Creator, Ruler, Judge, but as Father, Redeemer and Reconciler in Christ. Hence the weapons of its warfare must not be carnal, according to the wisdom of this world, but spiritual, according to the mind of God. Temporary defeats in this conflict, wherever and whenever it may be witnessed, there may be; but final disaster never, for the Church has the

certainty of God's promise which, as this chapter
has been so much concerned with the land of
Luther, may be expressed in his hymn.

> "With force of arms we nothing can,
>   Full soon were we down-ridden:
> But for us fights the proper man
>   Whom God Himself hath bidden.
>   Ask ye, Who is this same?
>   Christ Jesus is His Name.
>   The Lord Sabaoth's Son:
>   He, and no other one,
>   Shall conquer in the battle.
>
> .   .   .   .   .
>
> God's word, for all their craft and force,
>   One moment shall not linger,
> But, spite of hell, shall have its course;
>   'Tis written by His finger.
>   And though they take our life,
>   Goods, houses, children, wife,
>   Yet is their profit small;
>   These things shall vanish all,
>   The city of God remaineth."

(5) While sincerely sympathising with, and
cordially appreciating the Confessional Church
in Germany in its struggle for the independence
of the Church, we must in candour admit
that it is concern for the Gospel, which is the
primary motive, and not interest in religious
liberty, and that the wider interest of *personal*
liberty has not been considered.

(*a*) And yet if we take the view of religion

which is assumed in this volume—the relation of the whole man to the whole reality of God in His world—we must hold that the Church cannot ignore nor neglect this wider interest. Civilisation and culture are not departments of human activity to which the Church can be indifferent. It is the will of God that men shall be fed, clothed, sheltered, kept in health—in short in physical well-being; it is no less (if not more) His will that they shall have the opportunity of developing their capacity for the realisation of the ideals of truth, goodness, beauty and love. In the economic sphere the Church must resist any interference with personal liberty which is arbitrary, because unnecessary to secure the common economic interests, to promote social solidarity on the level of the adequate supply of legitimate physical needs. Hence I have never been able to commit myself to theoretical Socialism, although ready to approve such social-isation of the possession and control of industry as may be necessary to protect the economically weak against exploitation by the economically strong, and to secure the adequate supply just mentioned. I believe in " the inevitableness of gradualness," God's method of working. An illustration, which just because of its grotesqueness may leave a more permanent impression, may be excused. At a church-meeting it was decided

K

to use the material of the old building for the new, and to occupy the old building till the new was ready. That physical impossibility is an analogy of a social possibility. We cannot pull down one economic system, and build up another, but the pulling down and the building up of the same material must go together, and there must be continuous use. The value of an economic system should be estimated by the measure in which it preserves personal liberty as well as the extent to which it promotes material interests. A poorer nation of free men is to be preferred to a richer nation of slaves. I do not say the two aims are incompatible, but indicate what my choice would be in the interests of man as personal. Nor is this a plea for the present economic order, which limits personal liberty more injuriously than a collectivist system probably would, for now the enslavement is for private gain, then it would be for the public good. Nevertheless in the extension of the functions of the State in this sphere a vigilant scrutiny must be exercised lest in the winning of the world the soul be lost.

(b) Still more in the sphere of culture in the widest sense is freedom essential to satisfaction and progress. While the State may, and ought to, encourage and support science, philosophy, art, morals, associations for cultural ends by providing elementary, secondary, and university education, laboratories, libraries, art-galleries, etc., it would be desirable that there should be the largest liberty possible in administration, so long as the public task is discharged, and not sacrificed to any private interests. As dangerous and disastrous as the assault on the Church in Germany is the attempted subordination of all cultural interests to the policy of the State. The treatment of eminent scholars and thinkers in the Universities for political reasons is a shameful abuse of the power of any Government. The position of the churches in Italy is precarious, but even more than in Germany it would seem the effort is being made to use culture entirely as a means to the end of Fascism. Not only should the Church be ready to co-operate with all cultural interests and associations which are combating this pernicious tendency, but on it falls a special responsibility for leadership. It is concerned, as has been said, with the whole man, to whom in Christ, because Christ is God's, all things belong (I Cor. iii. 23), and it is not protecting an alien interest in setting the battle in array on so wide a front. God has entrusted man with the precious and perilous dowry of personal liberty; he can fulfil personality only in the exercise of liberty in " self-knowledge, self-reverence, self-control," and the Church is about its own task, in guarding that divine gift against arbitrary human encroachments.

(c) It is to be feared that the Church has laid itself open to the reproach that it is concerned about liberty only when its own independence is threatened, and even that it has been only too ready to invoke the interference of the State to prevent what it disapproved. For instance, while the State must have a concern for morals, and there are moral evils, prostitution, drunkenness, betting and gambling which in the interests of the community it must restrain; there is a tendency among many good Christian people to ask the State to stop whatever they do not like; there is a form of Puritanism more zealous about preventing evil than promoting good. That there must be some restraint when the common conscience requires it, and that the Church may appeal for that restraint may be admitted as legitimate principles, but in their application there must be reserve, " the wisdom of the serpent " as well as " the harmlessness of the dove." There may be an expression of atheism so offensive to the general sentiment that common decency demands some restraint on blasphemy, but on the whole it seems to me the Church should never press for the enforcement of antiquated blasphemy laws; and it must also observe the obligation of con-

sideration and courtesy in dealing with " free-
thought " which it expects for itself. In the
censorship of books, films, plays, this same
wise moderation must be shown. The action
of the State in the restraint of folly and wickedness is necessary; an unregenerated society is
still under law, and not under grace; but
the Church, as the herald of grace, will seek
to replace the restraints of law as fully and as
fast as it can by the constraints of love. Compulsion is forbidden by its very end; persuasion is its only means; for men are not to
be subjugated to obedience to God, but eman-
cipated by the grace of Christ into the love of
God. The ecclesiastical organisation is no end
in itself, but only a means of the Church—as
the object and the organ of the Kingdom of
God; and the kingdom of God is no arbitrary
exercise of God's omnipotence, but the free
saving activity of the Fatherhood, the filial
service of God which alone is perfect freedom.

(6) From the theological standpoint of this
volume, the State is to be regarded as not existing
of or *for* itself, as possessing the attributes of
God alone, *aseity* or *proseity*; it has not its *source*
or its *purpose* in itself. Whatever the historical
antecedents of States may be, their source is
in *community*, man as social personality by divine
endowment and appointment, as possessing com-

mon interests and activities, and as giving effect to them in *association* with his fellow-men. Whatever purpose human avarice, ambition and arrogance may have assigned to States, their purpose, as God wills it, is to secure and maintain that association which expresses that community. A State approaches the ideal as its authority rests not on force, although it may use force in the last resort against human folly or wickedness, but on the consent of its citizens, who loyally participate in its functions, because in their exercise it is faithfully fulfilling its purpose. The only legitimate political interest there is—if we may speak of such an interest by itself—is that it discharges its functions efficiently with the assent of those whom it exists to serve. Even to make the nation, of which the State is the organ, an end in itself, is an insult to God, who alone has *proseity*, and an injury to humanity, the mutual dependence and obligation of all nations to one another, that internationalism with which the last chapter will deal. However great a nation may be, it is idolatry to put it in the place of God; and however worthily a State may function it is irreverence to put it on an equality with the Church, for the bounds of the one are temporal, and of the other the eternal.

(7) So manifold are the functions of the State that it has been generally recognised that the present organisation of the State is not adequate for efficiency. In view of this complexity, Rudolf Steiner has advocated an organ for each of its functions, economic, cultural and political. How far such a separation would be practicable is too large a question to be now discussed. Some central authority there must be; this would be the political, but there might possibly be advisory and auxiliary to it an economic and a cultural Council, the membership of which would, however, need to include not only those specially competent and interested, but also those of wider outlook animated only by the common good. While integration must be preserved, there must be differentiation. If this consideration be true, the " totalitarian " state is an anachronism, a reversion to earlier and lower types of the State now out of date, and not an advance in the way of progress.

(1) IF what has been maintained in previous chapters is true—namely, that the extension of the functions of the State has been, not only inevitable, but even desirable, that the expansion of the mission of the Church to be totalitarian, to bring all the kingdoms of this world into captivity to the Kingdom of the Son of God's love is imperative, and that the spheres of Church and State are consequently overlapping in greater measure, the conclusion must be drawn, that if this intimate relation is not to be an occasion of conflict, such as the previous chapter has described, a method of co-operation must be devised by a recognition of complementary and not conflicting purposes.

(a) Several more general considerations may lead us to that recognition. As God is one, and in Him there is no variation, or shadow that is cast by turning (James i. 17), the distinction of Creator, Preserver, Ruler must not be allowed to become artificial divisions, but all must be unified in the Christian conception of Father. His decrees as Creator before or after the Fall must be dismissed as abstract fictions, and all God's sovereign activity must be conceived as redemptive and reconciling.

(*b*) Accordingly the State must not be excluded from the universal range of His purpose as Father to save and bless all mankind in Christ. That the State is a penalty for sin, and that its essence is force are perniciously false conceptions, which will stand in the way of any true and right view of the relation of Church and State. Just as in the cosmic and human evolution, there comes first the natural, and then the spiritual, the psychic man as the preparation for the pneumatic (I Cor. xv. 44, 45), so the discipline of law precedes the disclosure of grace. Moses came before Christ (John i. 17) and in Israel as in other nations the State preceded the Church, or rather there was one Church-State. The Church as a distinct and separate community of faith emerges only when a religiously creative personality advances in his religious consciousness beyond the beliefs, rites and customs of the nation, and gathers a group of disciples around him, *e.g.* Isaiah's remnant, Jeremiah's new covenant, the Christian *ecclesia* as the true Israel.

(*c*) But just as vital processes do not supersede physical and chemical in the living body, and as mind retains brain as its organ, so the Church does not annul the State. If the Christian believer is not under law, but under grace, he is not without law, for Christ becomes his motive and his standard. In so far as a man is not transformed by grace, he is still conformed to law. The bringing of society fully under the constraint of the love of Christ is a very gradual development; and the principles of Christ cannot be at once translated into practice without any regard to the limitations which the historical conditions impose. The Church must work for peace in the relation of the nations to one another; but it is altogether doubtful whether *pacifism*, individual or corporate, is the swiftest and surest method for attaining that end. Because necessarily the ends and the means of the State fall short of the purpose and the method of the Church, the Church must not suspect the State as an enemy, but may welcome the State as an ally. Men need to be restrained from folly and wickedness until they can be constrained to wisdom and goodness. The outward compulsion may serve as a preparation for the inward impulsion. Law becomes a tyranny only when it is continued beyond its necessity, and prevents a liberty for which an individual or a community is prepared.

(*d*) From this consideration two obligations follow, the one negative and the other positive.

The Christian Church must not, as some extreme
doctrinaires, fanatically possessed by one idea,
would urge it to do, place itself in opposition
to the State, disobey its laws or challenge its
authority unless there is an overmastering constraint of a reflective conscience, and it must
duly weigh the consequences of the measure
of anarchy which its action might involve.
A later chapter will discuss some of the problems of the Christian conscience. Further, the
Christian Church must give all the encouragement and help which it can give to the State
in the discharges of all those higher functions
which promote the common good.

(2) The Church cannot expect to " sublimate "
the functions of the State to be an adequate
and consistent realisation of the Christian ideal,
but it can aim at so infusing the Christian
spirit into the activities of the State as to make it
a *præparatio evangelica*, or John the Baptist
preparing the way of the Lord (Matt. iii. 3).
To assume because of the present tension and
even conflict, due to abnormal conditions, that
there must be a permanent " incompatibility of
temper " between Cæsar and Christ is to ignore
the real gains of the past in humanising and
even Christianising government, and to distrust
the sufficiency of divine grace for human need,
the cleansing, renewing and hallowing influence

of the Spirit of God. In this enterprise " to doubt would be disloyalty, to falter would be sin."

(*a*) The way which the Christian Church has hitherto recognised, but not as constantly followed, is to encourage, and even summon Christian men and women individually to accept their responsibility as citizens; to use their vote so as to return representatives to local councils, or to the national parliament, who will carry on administration or support legislation which the Christian conscience can approve. No Christian minister is trespassing on ground he should avoid, who prior to any election calls attention to the obligation of Christian men and women to vote according to their conscience, not from partisanship or for expediency. When I was a pastor, I used to remind the congregation that the secret ballot offered them no protection from the scrutiny of Christ, and that in putting their cross opposite any name they should remember His Cross. I am sure that these words were not putting the matter on too high grounds. Some of our newspapers probably exercise more influence on many Christians at an election than does the Sermon on the Mount.

(*b*) There are Christian men and women who should not be content with voting for representatives, but should feel the obligation of offering themselves as representatives, whether for local councils or parliament. So many and so varied in quality are the motives of men and women in seeking office that there is need for the Christian motive of service to raise the level of our public life At Westminster a man or woman may be rendering necessary and effective service to the Kingdom of God.

(c) While the extension of the functions of the State can be welcomed, there is one qualification which must be added. The value of the administration will depend on the character and the spirit of the agents of the State. Official action may be dehumanised and become mechanical. A warder in a prison, an attendant in an asylum, a nurse in a hospital, a probation officer in a court may need to submit to regulations, to which individual philanthropy may not be subject, and may thus be unable to give full effect to the impulses of the Christian heart ; but nevertheless there is the opportunity of regarding these offices not merely as a means of livelihood, but as a ministry of Christian love. That love in act may do what that same love is not free to do in word : there may be restraints on religious propaganda in public institutions, but no rules can hinder the influence of consistent Christian personality. But there are also institutions, the purpose of which would not be betrayed, but fulfilled, if that influence directly aimed at moral recovery, through religious conversion. Even punishment should be reformatory; and the service of human need may be a means of Christian witness. Christian young men and young women should set aside the motives of ambition or avarice, and face the question, whether their vocation as Christians is not to be found in some such form of public service.

(*d*) For the full efficiency of the functions of the State there is not only needed this official service, but there is room for, and a call to voluntary co-operation. There is less suspicion than there was among officials of such allies. Voluntary effort cannot supersede, but it may supplement the public services. Even should the tendency to replace voluntary philanthropy by such services, as, for instance, in hospitals, increase, there is much that will still need to be done to express fully the Christian spirit of services freely rendered not as an official duty, but as a self-chosen bearing of the burdens of others. It would be a spiritual loss if no place could be found for the practice of neigh-bourly love, because the State had usurped all the functions of philanthropy. As the lump of State activity increases there is more and more need of the leaven of the Kingdom of God in Christian service to pervade it and transform it, so as to fulfil God's fatherly will.

(3) In this co-operation with the State, the State remains " the predominant partner," and the Church, unless when conscience forbids, should be prepared to comply with the regulations which the State, in the interests of the community to secure efficient and economical administration, may impose: it must not be a busybody meddling needlessly. On the other hand, however, the Church will not fulfil her vocation as the object and the organ of the Kingdom of God, the saving sovereignty of the Father, unless, while in her *sociological* aspect as a human society, holding property, administering funds, appointing and dismissing persons, generally making contracts, she must accept the laws of the land, she in her *soteriological* aspect as agent of God's purpose must not only assert her independence of the State, but even a superiority to the State as exponent of the mind and will of God, censuring if need be the action of the State when wrong, summoning the State to action when necessary for the common good, which includes character as well as condition, and advising the State as to the application of the principles of the Divine Revelation to

the concrete situation of the nation at the time. The Church has not only an apostolic function in proclaiming the Gospel of the grace of Christ for man's salvation, but also a prophetic function to read " the signs of the times," to trace the divine purpose and providence in the course of events, and to instruct the nations and their rulers in the ways of the Lord in which they should walk to avoid the curse of disobedience and to secure the blessing of submission to God's will. This to many who think the Christian religion to be a private interest, an individual concern, and the Church to be a voluntary association, with no more authority than other educational and cultural associations, may seem a preposterous arrogance; and the churches in their " whispering humbleness " by not claiming, and in their cowardly fear of man by not fulfilling their function lend countenance to this depreciation. The history of the past, in which hierarchical ambition and avarice claimed for the human society itself and its rulers a temporal sovereignty which was a challenge to national independence and individual liberty also has given ground for suspicion of, and antagonism to what appears unjustified interference in the affairs of this world. What I am pleading for here is not a privilege, but a responsibility; not an exaltation over men, but a submission to God, and I hope to show adequate reasons for my contention.

(a) What follows will have no validity or value for those who hold an agnostic, atheistic, secularist, or humanist standpoint; I have elsewhere dealt fully with the to me convincing evidence of the existence, nature, character and purpose of God; and may refer my readers who want to pursue the subject to my book on *The Christian Belief in God*. Here I assume the standpoint of Christian theism, as my argument is directed to those who are within the Christian Church, but may not share my conviction regarding the function of the Church. God as Creator, Preserver, Ruler, Father, is in all and through all as well as over all; from Him, for Him, and unto Him are all things. His authority is absolute and supreme; and men, as dependent on Him, are under obligation to seek, to know, and to strive to do His will, and further His purpose. Any distrust or disobedience is sin, and falls under His judgment, not less real, because of His goodness and grace. " God is not mocked, for whatsoever a man soweth that shall he also reap " (Gal. vi. 7).

(b) God is not a God who has hidden Himself, although no man can by searching find Him out, but One Who has made Himself known.

L

Man has no concern with as he can have no knowledge of God's secret decrees, about which some theologians so confidently spoke. But God has revealed Himself to men; in some measure He is really found of all who sincerely seek Him; He made Himself ever more fully known to the Hebrew people, until He revealed all that we may need for life and death, duty and destiny in Jesus Christ Our Lord, who as Son knowing made God as Father known, and through whom God is redeeming men from sin, and reconciling them to Himself. This saving revelation of God is not concerned only with individual duty and destiny, as a dogmatic evangelicalism has often represented it; but is a world-wide purpose. " God all things in all men."

(c) Accordingly as all finite reality, all mankind depends on God's creative and preservative activity, so it is all under His dominion, and included in His saving purpose in Christ. With the universality of the divine revelation and the human redemption in Christ I shall more fully deal in the last chapter. All that here must be maintained as a necessary stage of the argument is this, that there is no sphere of human interest or activity which falls outside of God's absolute supreme authority as Father, and not only as Creator. Human industry and human government are not subject to a Natural Law of God as Creator, distinct and separated from the grace of God as Father, redeeming and reconciling in Christ. To these spheres there does not belong the autonomy which has sometimes been claimed for them by non-theologians, and conceded by theologians. While I have learned a great deal, and hope to learn more from Continental Protestantism, its dualism is intolerable to me, for it appears transparently false. There is not a sphere of human society, unrelated to, and independent of the sphere of divine grace. In economics and in politics we are concerned with men, toiling and ruling; and they are to be redeemed from sin, and reconciled unto God in their whole manhood in all their relations.

(d) How is this revelation and salvation, so universal in its scope, to be made available for all men in all lands and all ages? The record of it is in the Holy Scriptures which preserve and diffuse the knowledge of the truth and grace of God. But not all who read can understand, and the numerous and often fantastic sects, into which Protestantism, especially American, is divided are a proof that the Bible needs to be interpreted for each people and each age; and Jesus left behind Him a society, to whom He promised the guidance of the

Spirit. The unity and the continuity of the Church have been broken by heresy and schism; and there is now not one ecclesiastical organisation which can claim to be alone the infallible interpreter. But, despite all the differences and divisions, all the follies and failures of men, the Guiding Spirit has not forsaken the churches (alas, that one should need to use the plural): there has been a communion of saints, seers, and sages. Candid minds and sincere hearts are not left in despair, as if the treasure of truth and grace had been altogether lost. I venture to believe that the Church (which is in all the churches) has growing resources of scholarship which enable it to understand the Bible as it has never been understood before; that a succession of prophets, not known by that name, and not acknowledged as such, have been reading the signs of the times, and have been tracing the Divine Providence in the confusions and conflicts of the world to-day; and that the Church has a wider vision, and can speak with a clearer voice about the Kingdom of God than previous generations, of whose labours and sufferings we are reaping the fruits. There has been sufficient progress in our understanding of Christian ethics as well as Christian theology, to justify the conviction that the Church ought, and the anticipation that it can, discover the mind of the Lord, and speak His Word for the world to-day.

(4) So much for the necessity and the possibility of the Church's witness to God; the actuality presents difficulties and discouragements which in candour must be stated.

(a) The Church as it is is far from being fit and worthy to be God's prophet, although it does not lack solitary prophetic voices. How much more authoritative, however, would the witness be if there were the united voice of the whole Christian community! As in the first so in the present generation, Christians have needed Paul's exhortation: " Be not fashioned according to this world; but be ye transformed by the renewing of your mind, that ye may prove what is the good and acceptable and perfect will of God " (Rom. xii. 2). The Church has made a compromise with the world, of which its duty is to be the monitor and counseller in the higher things; and its own thought and life has not risen much above the common level; and what is the more distressing is that it is not conscious of how far it is compromised. Troeltsch has shown to how great an extent Calvinist ethics have been affected by capitalist economics.[1] The

---

[1] *Op. cit.*, pp. 641–650.

current Christian morality takes the existing economic system for granted as God's will for industry and commerce, and tries to make the best of it, and never thinks of challenging its fundamental principle of self-interest as the dominant motive and competition as the prevalent method of business. The misery which that system may involve for many is accepted as an inevitable necessity to be met, not by any change in the system, but by the philanthropy which the surplus wealth of its favoured ones makes possible without great sacrifice. One wonders how far the lavish gifts of some millionaires to charity and other public interests are " a sop to the Cerberus " of an uneasy conscience. But wealth well-spent does not atone for wealth ill-gotten. So also Nonconformity in its struggle for toleration acquired a distrust of the activity of the State, and so favoured the principle of *laissez-faire*, where direction and control were imperative to protect the weak against wrongs. The prevalent tendency of the Christian churches has been an acquiescence in principle and practice in the economic and political spheres which a sensitive Christian conscience would have condemned.[1]

(*b*) It is this moral compromise which has

---

[1] See my book, *Can Christ Save Society?*

led many of the leaders of the Church even to justify as an obvious duty what on closer scrutiny is seen to be a dereliction of duty. The Christian minister with a clearer and wider vision, when he dares to pass it on, is told: " It's not your business to meddle with business," " Keep politics out of the pulpit." It would be difficult to persuade prominent and influential laymen that Mammon as well as Christ had been guiding their conscience and controlling their conduct. Less now than hitherto a man might become a suspect if he interested himself in, and preached about this Social Problem. The crisis in industry, commerce, politics, international relations, which is causing so much distress, danger, and despondency everywhere, and leading many to turn to strange and sorry physicians for the healing of their wounds, is a judgment on the Church as well as the world, for too often and too much in its testimony and its influence it has been fashioned according to this world, and has not been so transformed as to be wise enough to discern and brave enough to declare God's will.

(c) But God's judgment is also God's mercy; penalties may become opportunities, and perils promises. The Church has been frightened out of its complacency. The leaders who played for safety are less trusted; the wise and the bold are being listened to as not before. The calamity of the War has convinced many that " there is something rotten in the state " of the world; and the peace movement is gaining ground. But it is a fatal folly to sentimentalise about international friendship as a condition of peace, and leave undetected and unremoved the causes of friction, very largely economic. Reduction of armaments may make the temptation to an aggressive policy less, but reduced armaments may still be used, if the provocations of war are not also lessened. Even business men and politicians are beginning to have uneasy consciences, and to recognise the inadequacy of many of their economic and political expedients in a world unchanged in heart. The success of their various devices, welcome as on other grounds it might be, might prove a moral and religious loss, if it restored the former compromise and complacency in the world and the Church.

(d) If the Church is to offer the guidance which the world needs, it must recognise what is involved in Paul's distinction between being under law and under grace. Jesus is not a second Moses, nor the Sermon on the Mount a second Decalogue, even although the author of the First Gospel, a Jew writing for Jews, represents it as being so. The author of the Fourth

Gospel corrects that error, when he declares, that the law was given by Moses, "grace and truth came by Jesus Christ" (John i. 17). What this distinction means I have tried fully to explain in my book, *Can Christ Save Society?* I can simply state it here. The Christian ideal of life, as presented by Jesus, is the goal towards which the Church as the guide of human society must move, but it is not a law to be literally, immediately obeyed. The Christian conscience, under the guidance of the Spirit, must apprehend what is the *maximum* application of that ideal, which all the conditions of the moral situation allow and demand; the practicable is alone the obligatory. The individual Christian is not required to obey the precept of non-resistance literally (Matt. v. 38–42) without taking into account the whole moral requirements of equal love to self and neighbour at the time and the place and the personal relations. While he may be at liberty to sacrifice his own life, is it right for him to allow other lives to be sacrificed, if his resistance can preserve them? If the sacredness of human personality forbids injury to the assailant, does it not still more require the protection of the assailed? I do not ask the reader to assent to this particular application; but only to consider that literal obedience is not necessarily the only duty, and reflexion must be accepted as also a duty, so that the best in the moral situation may be done. Because the Christian must realise this ideal in a world, often non-moral and anti-moral, his fulfilment of the principles must fall short of the maximum conceivable and must aim at the maximum practicable; for he must consider not only the consequences for himself, but also the consequences for others. There are dangers of casuistry in seeking to reduce the ideal to the measure of personal inclinations and interests. That is *opportunism*, a moral infidelity. There is danger also in an unreflective morality, which allows itself to be guided by particular precepts, and does not with as wide a vision as is possible regard on the one hand the moral ideal in its entirety, and on the other the moral situation as a whole.

(*e*) There is one general consideration which must govern all the demands the Church makes upon the State. Not all citizens are members of the Church, and many would not accept the Christian ideal as their goal, or the Christian conscience as their guide; and consequently the principles of Christ cannot be carried out in the State as they ought to be, but alas! are still far from being in the Church. The State as it now is in the historical situation in which it finds itself, cannot be required to conform completely to the Sermon on the Mount, nor can it be condemned for not so doing. We must avoid on the one hand the acquiescence in the *status quo*, which from Luther onwards has been the weakness of, and can be brought as a reproach against Lutheranism, and on the other the ecclesiastical tyranny which Calvin sought to impose on Geneva, and which has given to Calvinism a harshly legal character. The obligations of the Christian individual and of the Christian community are the *maximum practicable*, as has just been shown; and the Church, individually and corporately, should be a challenging example, and, if need be, a humbling rebuke to general society. As Christ came for judgment into the world (John ix. 39), so the saints as reflecting and reproducing His likeness must ever judge the earth (I Cor. vi. 2). Further, it must not only by its testimony seek to grow as the mustard plant, by winning converts out of the world, but also by its influence as the leaven permeate, as far as the medium allows, the whole lump of society (Matt. xiii. 31–33), enlightening, cleansing and strengthening public opinion and popular sentiment, so that its demands on the State shall not be impracticable, but practicable, because the community has been prepared to desire or at least to accept them. The State has the responsibility of not merely following where the community leads it, but of itself leading as fast and as far as it will be followed; for, as representative of the nation, the Government cannot defy the nation's judgment and desire, and may yet stimulate it to advance. A Government which has the next election in view, and plays for safety, has betrayed its trust, and deserves the Church's remonstrance and rebuke; a Government which takes risks to meet the national situation as best it can, is one which deserves the Church's encouragement and support.

(f) In the measure in which the Church is divided, is its authority weakened, and even its right to speak lessened. A small section has no right to hinder the Church's testimony and influence, although Christian considerations must, as far as is consistent with the wider obligations, be shown; but where convictions are generally shared, and their expression is for the common good, the coward cry, "No politics in the pulpit," can and should be disregarded. As a general rule the necessary agreement will be confined to the ends rather than the means of action. The Church may apply the supreme law of equal love to neighbour and self to the present crisis in insisting that the paradox of *poverty amid plenty* must cease,

that there must be such a distribution of wealth
as will provide a decent standard of living for
all, as will end the scandal of wealth being
wasted that prices may be maintained, as will
encourage a consumption which will justify
the fullest use of the world's productive capacity.
That is sound economics as well as good ethics.
The Church corporately is not justified in
making any authoritative declaration, when it
is still divided in opinion, or its ideal gives
no immediate guidance as to the best means
for these ends. To identify either individualism
or collectivism with Christianity is unwarranted
presumption, although the moral advantages
or disadvantages may well be subjected to
the searching scrutiny of the Christian conscience. To regard the Douglas Credit scheme
as a divine oracle, which the Church must
deliver on pain of being denounced as " a dumb
dog that will not bark " is mischievous folly.
A black, red, brown or green shirt is not the
necessary badge of Christian wisdom, righteousness or love. So as regards war, to promote
peace by the cultivation of international friendship and co-operation, to prevent war by the
advocacy of arbitration and conciliation in
international disputes or of the largest measure
of disarmament which the nations can be in-
duced to accept by international agreement,

to urge the acceptance fully of the obligations which the Covenant of the League of Nations imposes, or any other treaties or pacts which aim at mutual protection against aggression, seem to me aims about which the Christian Church cannot be indifferent or inactive, but must be insistent in pressing as an obligation on the State. Even if I myself held the pacifist position, and felt bound to advocate it as an obligation on all Christians, I should not regard it as a duty to require the State also to become pacifist, or even to disarm unilaterally as a gesture to other nations. These may serve as illustrations of the limitations which the Church must recognise as moral guide of the State. In the next chapter I shall consider in more detail the pacifist position and the tension which must arise between the Christian conscience and the State because of the inevitably only partial realisation of the Christian ideal possible to it.

(g) Although the next consideration I now offer is implicit in what has just been said, it may be made explicit in a few sentences. The Church must make itself competent by adequate knowledge of all the relevant facts to offer sound judgment. It need not be an expert in economics or politics, or in the technique which action in these spheres may demand. But it should know enough not to offer advice, which may be regarded in both senses of the word as impertinent. Such incompetence affords an only too welcome excuse for disregard of its rebukes or counsels, and even denial of its authority. But if it is God's world, it is only His will that can avert disaster, and secure benefit in the ways and works of men. And there is no other human agency through which God's voice should be so clearly heard as through the Church, guided by the Spirit, and on earth the body of Christ.

(5) This co-operation with the State to be fully Christian must be tolerant, considerate, courteous. The Church should fully recognise the difficulties which confront, the dangers which threaten, the responsibilities which rest upon the State. It must not offer sentimental advice about the treatment of criminals, which would weaken the authority of the State in restraining crime. It must not urge extreme measures of disarmament which would prevent the State's exercising the international influence which its position and resources allow it, or fulfilling the pledges which it has made to other nations. It must not ask for economic changes which would jeopardise the common interests

of all classes of society. But it must also show by its adequate knowledge its competent judgment. These conditions being fulfilled, politicians are not justified in resenting the advice of the Church as illegitimate interference. When the Churches took action in regard to the Coal Strike, an action which, if the Government had followed the lead given, might have averted disaster—Mr. Baldwin, unlike his usual self, allowed himself a sneer, that he was expecting the Association of British Industries to offer its counsel to the Church of England in regard to the Revised Prayer Book. One of the bishops very properly replied that if the Association mentioned had taken as constant an interest, and shown as adequate a knowledge in this matter as the representatives of the Churches could claim in that, the advice would be valued. Mr. Neville Chamberlain spoke resentfully of the request of the Archbishop of York regarding the restoration of the cuts in the assistance for the Unemployed, as if the disposal of the nation's resources were a monopoly of the Government, and not the nation's concern, articulate through responsible, competent persons. I refrain from any invidious comparison of the qualifications of the two men concerned. During the War the support of the churches was welcomed, and was given with a lack of reserve which many of the wisest and best now regret. There is no time when the Church's counsel is not needed, and there should be no time when it is not competent or not courageous enough to speak: " Thus saith the Lord."

M

(1) THE Church of Christ has its corporate witness and influence in regard to the human good and duty; but within the Church itself there is not necessarily uniformity of judgment; indeed, the wider the range of knowledge of human life, its needs and perils, and the more sensitive the conscience to the obligations thus imposed, the more likely will be differences of judgment.

(*a*) The majority of the members of the Church will exercise only what we may call a *judicial* conscience; they will accept the standards of the community, and will judge themselves right or wrong in their conduct by these standards. Few comparatively are those who have what we may call the *legislative* conscience, who are always scrutinising the accepted standards, are discovering their inadequacy to the moral situation, and are advancing to higher standards of more exacting obligation. This is the way in which moral progress is made, for after a time the community follows their lead. There are pioneers into the regions beyond of duty, and by and by the new territory they have explored comes to be occupied by many others. It is thus that all social reforms have been accomplished. This legislative conscience is not entirely *intuitive* : it may be that the new moral conviction comes as a flash of light ; but a closer scrutiny will show that just as a so-called sudden conversion has had its psychic antecedents so *reflexion* lies behind the intuition, reflexion both on the need and the means of meeting it which lie implicit, not yet explicit, in recognised general principles. The Christian conscience does not claim to be original; it is guided by the Spirit of God into a fuller application to the circumstances of the Christian ideal, as revealed in Christ, the eternal reality of God as love, whose perfection men as the children of God are called by His grace to reproduce. This ideal is not a code of law to be literally obeyed; but an ideal so broad and high that it can be only partially apprehended and applied to the varying circumstances of life. The Church as a whole is likely to be behind its moral seers, sages, and saints in its apprehension and application; but should respect them and guard them in the exercise of their liberty.

(*b*) The Church as a whole may be expected in its moral standards to be in advance of the current standards of society, and still more of the standards which guide the legislation and the administration of the State, as it is recognised that there is a sphere of private morals in which the State cannot interfere without becoming oppressive and in which it is in the interests of morality itself to recognise individual liberty and responsibility. Accordingly, besides the conflict between Church and State discussed in the fifth chapter, there are clashes of conscience and law on particular issues which deserve consideration. It must not be assumed that the law is always in the wrong, nor yet that even if conscience is right, it is always justified in resistance.

(i) There is a perverse and reactionary conscience as well as an enlightened and progressive. When the individual standard falls below the social standard as embodied in law, it may be the duty of the State to restrain and punish. The United States of America were justified in forbidding the polygamy of the Mormons; any community would be right in hindering the exhibitions of the nudists; the Raj in India has the more enlightened Indian opinion on its side in legislation against child-marriage, in previous prohibitions of widow-burning, and the cruelty of the car of Juggernaut. If India gains the self-government that is desirable, difficult questions will arise for the supreme authority, if any return to discarded standards is attempted. The individual conscience cannot be accepted as the ultimate moral authority, when it lags behind the moral advance already made by the community or in its government.

(ii) There are persons who have a " painful conscience," a pain to themselves, and to all with whom they are concerned. To be always " agin the Government " is not necessarily wisdom or virtue. So important is the respect for law and the preservation of order, that a clear and urgent imperative of conscience can alone justify disobedience or resistance; and as for the use of violence, that course seems to me to be wrong in a community where there exist the means of redress and reform. The Conservative Party brought moral disgrace upon itself in the measure in which it supported the resistance of Ulster to the proposed Home Rule legislation, even encouraging mutiny in the Army. To the methods adopted in the Women's Suffrage movement, it seems to me the Christian conscience could give no approval, only adverse judgment. It is well that the reform was not achieved by those methods; and that the vote came to women in recognition of their services and sacrifices for the nation during the War. I must here confess my own change of mind as regards *passive resistance* as a protest against the Education Act, which put the non-provided or denominational schools on the rates. My resistance was altogether passive; I observed every courtesy and gave every facility to the agents of the law who came to seize my goods in payment of the small fraction of the rate I had withheld; and I bought back these goods at an enhanced price. But I refused to join any organisation, or to take part in any propaganda, and was opposed altogether to the method adopted by some worthy, but mistaken, zealots in transferring their property to their wives, thus courting imprisonment. In view of the orgies of lawlessness witnessed in many parts of the world, I now judge that even what I then did was wrong; the injustice involved was not great enough to justify even that very mild defiance of law. The Labour Party discredited itself by the sanction it gave to the General Strike, which even success would not have justified. Much of the discredit of that calamity must fall also upon the Government, which, like Pharaoh of old, hardened its heart, and did not take measures to avert the conflict. No less of a moral iniquity was the " Black and Tan " policy of the Government, for Governments must avoid tyranny, if subjects are to be restrained from anarchy. The hardships involved in the law of Tithes call for removal, but the violent resistance to distraints, mistaken as the enforcement of the law in the circumstances may have been, cannot claim sympathy as an expression of the Nonconformist conscience. I have dealt so fully with these instances, as I am convinced that to-day the Christian Church and individual Christians must not lend any countenance to the weakening of the obligations of citizenship, respect for law, and the maintenance of order. No less, on the other hand, is the obligation of the Government to administer law and enforce order considerately, to offer speedy redress of proved wrong, to leave the largest measure of liberty to the individual conscience compatible with its obligations to the community, to avoid any provocations that would appear to justify resistance. In this connection how significant is the constant opposition of the prophets and of Jesus Himself to violent resistance of even oppressive governments.

(2) Some of the particular problems in which the Christian conscience and the law of the State may come into conflict may now be discussed.

(a) We begin with the fundamental social institution, the family. (i) The Christian standard of life-long love, devotion and fidelity in marriage must be maintained by the Church, and acceptance of that standard should be expected of all who seek the divine blessing on their union in the Christian ordinance. It cannot be required, however, that the State, in dealing with the legal contract in a community not wholly Christian, should conform its legalisation to that standard, and not allow other grounds of divorce than adultery. The suspicion which attaches to much of the evidence brought forward in the Divorce Courts, the almost legal compulsion to commit that sin, if intolerable bonds are to be severed, the evils arising out of legal separation without divorce, all supply moral grounds for a change of law. Whether the Church sanctions the marriage of divorced persons—guilty or innocent—by her ordinance is a domestic matter for the Church, with which the State should not interfere, for not every legal marriage can thus be recognised as a Christian marriage.

While the right of the Roman Catholic Church to enforce the *ne temere* decree on its own membership cannot be denied, although its expediency and "catholicity" may well be questioned, yet no priest should be entitled to describe a legal marriage as "living in sin," or its offspring as "bastards"; and if such language is used of an individual case, the law of libel should be invoked.

(ii) The Roman Church is also within its

rights in its opposition to the use of contraceptives, or the sterilisation of the unfit, and there are many Christians outside of that communion who share these convictions. A State would be unjustifiably challenging Christian consciences if it sanctioned the use of public clinics or other agencies of mother-aid as an agency for a propaganda in favour of birth restriction by such means, although it must allow the poor woman to have access to such medical knowledge as the rich woman has, if health interests are involved. Despite the Concordat, the German Government has challenged the authority of Rome by its law of compulsory sterilisation—in my judgment a wrong course. In our own land a Committee of the Home Office has reported in favour of voluntary sterilisation under proper safeguards. Probably most of our churches have never considered the question, and are, through this ignorance, incompetent to form a judgment. It is probable that they would not be able to agree on a common pronouncement for or against. But at least they should not allow themselves to be rushed into opposition, until they have duly considered the proposals and the evidence for them. Are they right in evading their responsibility in a matter of such importance if they are to sustain their claim to give moral guidance to society, and have they furnished themselves with the competent organ of witness? I myself cannot shirk the duty of stating that I cannot oppose the proposal made, and must add that those who are advised on medical grounds to submit to the operation should by some representative of the Church be instructed as regards the moral grounds for their acquiescence, so that their act shall have moral value as approved by conscience.

(*b*) From the home we can pass to the school. (i) As has already been argued, an education which excludes religion is not only a quantitatively incomplete, but a qualitatively defective education, as religion is not merely a subject to be taught along with other subjects; it is a spirit which should pervade the teaching of other subjects. I have sympathy with the insistence on a religious atmosphere, although the dogmatic ecclesiastical atmosphere often desired is for me not a help but a hindrance to the kind of religion which should prevail in education. I sympathise also with those who desire the religious instruction to be given by those who themselves believe what they teach, and can exercise a religious influence.

(ii) I recognise, however, as they do not, that schools, maintained by the community, not wholly Christian, and among the Christians even divided in doctrine and worship, should not enforce any religious tests on the teachers. The risk must be run of the religious instruction being given as a professional routine, and not a personal service, but in most schools provision could be made for relieving teachers who so desired of that duty. The Roman Catholic Church presents an insoluble problem as regards inclusion in any national system, and its schools would need to be granted exceptional treatment. But the more Christian relations of Anglicans and Nonconformists hold out the hope that their differences may be adjusted without the oppression of any conscience. So long as there is a conscience clause, exempting from religious instruction those children whose parents do not desire them to receive it, they have no adequate ground for complaint or resistance. If God be all that religion believes Him to be, the ultimate cause, the final purpose, the essential reality, the absolute authority, and if religion be the highest expression of human personality, it cannot be regarded as a private interest and no public concern, and if, as has been argued, consequently no education is adequate for the common good of the society unless it is religious, the majority who hold this conviction would be treated oppressively by the minority who do not share in it if forbidden by their objection to give effect to it as considerately for every scruple, as tolerantly for every difference as possible. So long as teachers are not required to teach, or scholars to learn what they do not believe, it seems to me, with all respect to the rights of conscience, religious instruction and influence have a rightful place in the education of youth. I am afraid the Free Churches, in their contention against sectarianism in education, have given the impression that religion was a desirable, but not necessary accessory of life which men might take or leave just as they pleased. The countries which have adopted secular education are recognising that the exclusion of religious instruction is a mistake.

(iii) That that instruction fails to be as competent and as effective as it needs to be must be conceded; but a hopeful feature of our times is the growing interest in its improvement, and the increasing readiness of the Churches, the teachers, and the education authorities to co-operate for this end. The necessity of general morality for the stability of the State, the common good of the community, is generally recognised; not so general, but not on that account less true, is the conviction that the most constraining motive, and the most sustaining power for morality is to be found in religion, not as an external sanction by rewards and punishments, but as an internal source of motive and power.

(c) After school comes the earning of the daily bread; from the domestic and educational sphere youth passes to the economic. In that sphere itself many problems of conscience emerge. (i) If, as I believe, in this sphere there are deep-rooted moral evils—self-interest as too dominant a motive, and competition as too prevalent a method, the man who tries to live by the Christian ethics will experience a constant tension between what he needs to do to hold his own in that sphere, and what he ought to do as a Christian disciple, and many Christian men are recognising this tension, and are prepared to subject the economic system to critical scrutiny. The excuse that " business is business " is itself an accusation; for there should not be any sphere of human life and work to which the Christian standards should not be applicable. A book like Wilder's *Heaven's My Destination*, in which the hero makes many blunders and gets into all sorts of scrapes by trying to live and act as the Christian ethics, taken literally, requires, and so to the world appears a fool, yet to the discerning reader is disclosed as " God's fool," challenges the moral bases of modern society, especially in the economic sphere. In the severity of the struggle involved a ruthless hardness supplants Christian love, and men feel themselves compelled in self-preservation to disregard the interests of others, even to inflict injury upon them. Instead of the result of "every man for himself" being "God for us all," it has proved to be "the devil take the hindmost." A State which does not recognise this inherent contradiction to Christian morals in this dominant motive and prevalent method of industry and commerce, and even shapes its policy in accordance with "economic nationalism," instead of seeking to direct and control, so far as the State can without undue interference with individual liberty and with due recognition of "the inevitableness of gradualness" in any transition from one economic order to another, in order to bring about a better system, is challenging the more sensitive and progressive Christian conscience of many to-day. There may be temporary compromise as a less evil in regard to the real interests of the community than resistance, but a permanent concord between God and Mammon there cannot be (Matt. vi. 24).

(ii) Apart from these moral evils in the system itself, and yet consequent on them, there are practices which, if not illegal, offend the Christian conscience when its sensitiveness has not been blunted. It is significant that recently a conference of young people asked that the Christian Social Council should offer guidance to them in their perplexities and difficulties, when they were expected to do what they believed a Christian ought not to do. There seems to be need of legislation against many of the scandals which are from time to time brought to light. Could the law provide adequate compensations for dismissal of an employee because he refused to conform to wrong practices? This is no Quixotic proposal, but deserves fuller examination by the churches, as it cannot be the real interest of any community that the morals of its youth should be corrupted by dishonesty or injustice, no less than by the generally condemned vices. The purpose of this volume forbids the pursuit of the problems in the economic sphere, which are not connected with the legislation or administration of the State. The battle on this field is not yet fully joined, as the churches generally have not yet recognised the magnitude or the urgency of the problem, and still cherish the illusion that business is not their business, and that Christian men need no authoritative guidance how here, as in all else, they may walk in God's ways. It would be well for the world if Christian men were as concerned here about what the Spirit is saying to-day to the Churches as they are beginning to be about the danger of war and the duty of peace.

(d) The late War found the Christian Churches unprepared morally for the issue then raised, although there were a few forward-looking men who saw the peril coming, and were making efforts to avert it. The first conference of the World Alliance for Promoting International Friendship through the Christian Churches met at Constance on the very eve of the War in 1914, and some of the delegates found difficulty in getting home after its outbreak. (i) Although the question of the conscientious objector, who refuses to have any participation in war as a combatant is usually in the forefront in these discussions, yet, in my judgment, this is beginning at the wrong end. The primary duty of the Churches is by the promotion of the internationalism, which will be dealt with in the next chapter, to bring about such conditions, economic and political, within each nation, and between the nations, as will encourage friendship, and maintain peace by meeting legitimate national needs, and prevent war by removing the provocations to it—in short, a condition in the world in which no Christian man will need to ask himself: Can

I as a Christian fight? Further, the Christian churches should not be content with
affirming generally that war is contrary to the
spirit and method of the divine revelation and
human redemption in Christ, but should frankly
recognise that such an affirmation raises one
of the most acute problems which the Christian
conscience can face and must not shirk: must
this general principle be applied without any
exception in all circumstances? I envy the
confidence with which many Christians can
answer, " Yes." I am not going to argue
whether it is my moral infirmity or my moral
discernment which makes me hesitate so confidently to give an answer. There is a revelation
of God in the course of human history, in the
moral order of the world, in the progress of
mankind, as the fulfilment of divine purpose;
and in it there is retribution as well as redemption, law as well as grace, judgment as well as
mercy, not we may as Christians believe as
final, but as preparatory and disciplinary; and
the end is not yet. " God is not mocked:
whatsoever a man soweth, that shall he also
reap " (Gal. vi. 7). If a man will not come
under grace, he remains under law; if a man
does not seek and find forgiveness, judgment
will fall upon him. So of nations, redemption
has not yet gained its final triumph; right

N

still needs to be vindicated and wrong resisted. Injustice, oppression, cruelty are evil as well as war, and a world which was restrained from war by fear of its horrors might be less worthy and fit morally than one which faced its sacrifices to put an end to these evils. It is only just to heroic Christian men, who counted not " their lives dear unto themselves " because they recognised a cause as worth dying for, that this possibility should be recognised.

(ii) What is to be hoped, prayed and worked for is that the League of Nations shall become authoritative enough to secure that what we may call private wars, corresponding to the duel of former days for individuals, wars of national self-interest, ambition or avarice or revenge, shall fall under universal judgment, and that the only permissible war shall be public war, corresponding within the nation to police, law-courts, prisons, etc., for individual transgressors, the sole purpose of which shall be to afford mutual security against any aggression. Patriotism, "my country right or wrong," affords no justifications for war, only resistance to wrong and vindication of right, the maintenance of a moral order in the world. Should the League of Nations fall under private interests, and prove an unjust judge, any measures it might take would no less fall under the judgment of the Christian conscience. It seems to me of primary importance that an international responsibility for the security of each nation should replace the right each nation now claims to defend its own interests. Whether this involves an international force, as some advocates of peace maintain, or reliance should solely rest on the pledge of each nation to come to the help of its neighbour, when attacked, by regional pacts within and not in rivalry with the League of Nations, is an alternative of policy about which the Churches should not make haste to come to any decision. A prominent pacifist has, I believe, come to the conclusion that an international force should be provided; I who cannot take the pacifist position have my doubts, lest the possession of the weapon ready at hand should prove a temptation to its speedy use before all other sanctions have been exhausted. My hatred of war is as intense as any pacifist's; but just as in philosophy to-day there is a tendency to idealist-realism, so in moral issues we must apply the general principle in view of all the circumstances, so that it shall have its maximum effect. The Churches would, it seems to me, be justified at any cost in opposing by their testimony and influence, with all the resources at their command any war, of which self-interest was the motive, any war in which all the means of arbitration or conciliation or judicial decision had not been used to the utmost limit, or in which an impartial judgment on the quarrel had been disregarded. Resistance to sudden aggression of any kind should not, in my reluctant judgment, fall under their condemnation. If such a policy were followed by the Churches, could they be charged with failure in their duty, disloyalty to Christ?

(iii) I have so high a regard for many who hold the pacifist position, and I think their witness is of such value as a constant challenge to an immoral acquiescence in the necessity of war, that I do not wish to enter into any controversy on the subject, although I must also admit that the persistence and even pugnacity with which some of them obtrude their views on all occasions has hindered as united a front of the Churches as the difficulty of the situation demands, and effective common action on a constructive peace policy. I have already given the reasons why I cannot take their position unreservedly, and need not pursue the argument further, except to add some observations. The pacifist appeals to the principle of the sacredness of human personality as forbidding any resistance which involves any injury of an assailant; he does not ask himself whether this same principle might not require the protection of the assailed. A man may, if the cause justifies that sacrifice, allow himself to be wronged or injured without resistance or redress; but it is a moral problem whether his responsibility for others justifies his allowing them to be sacrified without any effort to save. If a whole nation resolved to immolate itself on the altar of peace, the Government might be justified in bringing about total disarmament; but so long as a nation were not willing, the Government would be under moral obligations to provide the necessary protection. Further, if it had incurred obligations to other nations, it could not rightly throw off these obligations. That is the reason why I must oppose all proposals of *unilateral disarmament*. A Government may be required by the Christian conscience to do its utmost to promote peace and general disarmament, and not to increase its armaments at such time or such ways as would imperil these primary interests. Have all pacifists, eloquent on platforms, calmly and clearly considered the question whether they would wish the maxim on which they are acting to become a general law (to apply the Kantian test), and are they prepared to accept all the consequences to others as well as themselves? If they have, they show what I cannot but regard as reckless-ness. To expect God to work a miracle, either physical by preventing the terrible results of invasion, or moral by changing the heart of the assailant is, in my judgment, not faith, but presumption, corresponding to the second temptation of Our Lord, to which He answered, "Thou shalt not tempt the Lord thy God" (Matt. iv. 7). The Cross of Christ is sometimes appealed to as a sanction of such a gesture, as it is called. As regards the immediate result, which is what is expected, the Cross did not change the heart of mankind, and is only slowly triumphing over man's sin. The attitude expressed in the now historic phrase "Damn the consequences" is not, as I see it, a moral or a religious attitude. Assuredly we must do right at whatever cost, but what is right is not only an abstract principle, but the application under conditions of which we must take account.

It is painful for me to appear as the devil's advocate; but the Christian disciple must be "wise as a serpent" as well as "harmless as a dove," and he finds himself often as "a sheep among wolves" (Matt. x. 16). Is Jesus' warning: "Give not that which is holy unto the dogs, neither cast your pearls before swine, lest haply they trample them under their feet, and turn and rend you" (Matt. vii. 6) one to be disregarded, or to be taken and used with wisdom and charity? The redemptive order is not yet dominant in the world, although we must pray and labour for its triumph; but the retributive order of reaping according to sowing still holds sway, and we must not let hopes conceal facts in our judgments. It is the sense of shame and sorrow that in the world as it is grace cannot have free course, but that law must still restrain and chastise, which is what I understand to be the meaning of the experience of being crucified with Christ; but as Christians are so crucified will they also gain the assurance that there is a resurrection for mankind in Christ (Rom. vi. 8–10), although it must be after many days. To invoke divine omnipotence to solve the problems of this " sorry scheme of things " is not, so I have learned Christ, the Way, *sola gratia sola fide*.

(iv) But while I cannot hold the pacifist position myself, I recognise that it is not a reactionary morality which it represents, but a progressive, and that it is the business of the Christian Church to secure for it the largest possible measure of toleration. In this respect the Christian Churches of this country fell below their duty in not protesting vigorously enough against the brutalities which were inflicted on the pacifists who were refused exemption by the tribunals, most of them so constituted as to be quite unfit to decide on difficult and delicate questions of conscience, and in not bringing pressure upon the Government to change the method of dealing with such cases. Whether the national danger demanded conscription or not, the Act itself was falsely conceived and badly administered. The manhood of the nation should not have been placed, unless when exempted, in the hands of the military authorities, and not all conscientious objectors were fairly treated.

Those who applied for exemption should have remained under civil control; if not exempted they should have had alternative work offered to them, and even if they refused that, they might have had fine or imprisonment imposed upon them to purge their offence once for all, if that had seemed imperative for the nation's safety, so as to serve as a deterrent of others, although I myself do not think such penalty deserved. With these conscientious objectors who refused any alternative service I cannot agree, for they strained the rights of individual conscience to breaking point. Because a man disapproves of the national policy, he is not justified in refusing service against which in itself he can have no scruple, such as working on the land, tending the sick, teaching, etc. He is enjoying many benefits of citizenship, and he is not entitled to disown all its obligations, even if he objects to the policy of the Government. What confusion there would be, if Liberals refused to pay their taxes when a Conservative Government was in power! No man should pick a quarrel with his country unless in the most imperative necessity. Nevertheless even these extremists should have had a protection through the influence of the Churches which was not then given. There were comparatively few, even among the Free Churches, who were as concerned as they should have been. I once appealed to one of the ministers of the Crown, a Nonconformist, to put a stop to these outrages, and met only with contemptuous ridicule of my concern for them. Others with me approached the late Lord Kitchener a few days before the tragic close of his great career, and met with courteous consideration, and a frank recognition that conscientious objections ought to be respected.

(e) In the treatment of criminals, questions of conscience may arise. A judge may himself be convinced that the law which requires the sentence of death for murder, and does not discriminate in the degrees of guilt, ought to be amended, and yet it is the duty which his vocation imposes upon him that he shall pronounce the same sentence on all, although there may be some relief in the representations which he may make to the Home Secretary when there is an inquiry into the exercise of the Sovereign's prerogative of mercy. A jury-man may be opposed to capital punishment, but if the evidence is adequate to prove the accused guilty, he is not justified in refusing assent to the verdict. A man's official position may require him to do what, if he had no such responsibility, he would feel free to abstain from doing. A Scottish preacher, who was trying to justify some of the commands ascribed in the Old Testament to Jehovah, but now offensive to the Christian conscience, labouring under a sense of failure, added quaintly, even perhaps grotesquely, "My friends, God may have to do in His official capacity what He would be ashamed to do as a private indi-vidual." It sounds a very lame apology; but it has a core of truth. God, as sustaining the moral order of the world, allowing men to reap as they have sown, may be putting a restraint on His loving Heart as Father which is His eternal Cross; and social duty in one's own nation, or in the relation of nations, may sometimes compel men in the fulfilment of their responsibilities to share that cross in time. The relation between that retributive order and the redemptive which must be taken into account in these problems of war and criminal justice is the tragic mystery of the world, relieved in the Cross of Christ by the disclosure of the sacrificial, saving, vicarious love of God.

(3) There is a problem of conscience which arises from the relation which in most Protestant countries has prevailed between Church and State.

(a) It has been definitely affirmed elsewhere in this volume that the Church, to discharge fully its duty to society, must be independent of the State; and it does not seem altogether improbable that the experiences through which so many Churches are passing of oppression by the State will evoke that conviction even among those who have not held it hitherto, who have either remained indifferent in the matter, or have maintained a contrary opinion. In closing this chapter this problem must be faced. If, as has been argued, the spheres of Church and State cannot be separated, as the saying, " A free Church in a free State " seems to assume to be possible, and if the extension of the functions of the State and the expansion of the interests and activities of the Church involve that both will be on the same ground, e.g., education, although with different methods, but not necessarily contrary purposes, how close must be their co-operation if conflict

is to be avoided! Protestants must not forget
that the Papacy in the Middle Ages stood for
the independence of the Church, even its
superior authority to that of the State. The
claim was made too arrogantly, and often in
the interests of the hierarchy rather than those
of the Kingdom of God—indeed, both interests
were identified. One of the consequences of
the Reformation was that the churches of
Protestantism were brought into subjection to
the State, and these established churches still
exist. The Separatists in England, dissatisfied
with the slow progress of Reformation under
Queen and bishops, set themselves to fashion
a Church according to the New Testament
pattern as they understood it " without tarrying
for any." The Puritan—the more Protestant
element—was ejected from the Church of
England by the Act of Uniformity of 1662. Till
1789 there were laws to suppress Nonconformity. In Scotland, too, there were struggles
for " the Crown-Rights of the Redeemer "—
secessions and disruptions. Although the relation of the churches is becoming steadily, not
only more tolerant, but even appreciative and
co-operative, yet for the English Nonconformist
and the Scottish dissenter there remains the
problem of conscience; how far must he oppose
the Established Church, not as a Church, but

as established, or can he acquiesce in its existence?

(b) As a Scotsman by nationality and nurture, I hope I shall not be regarded as impertinent if I express my judgment that the problem has found a reasonable and acceptable solution in the Constitution of the National Church of Scotland. As an English Nonconformist by adoption I recognise that there are privileges and benefits of the Church of England which are contrary to the religious equality before the law of all citizens, and that some even inflict injustices and injuries. It is no lack of esteem for the Church of England to be vigilant for the prevention of wrongs and the redress of grievances. So unlike is the relation of Church and State in England to that in Scotland that it would seem to me a mistake to assume that what has been accomplished in Scotland could with equal ease be brought about in England. I myself regretted, and even incurred some odium by opposing, the intervention of the Nonconformist Churches in the controversy about the Prayer-Book. That humiliation has led many Anglicans to desire the independence of the Church, but few would be ready to assent to such a measure of Disendowment as would appear to be a necessary accompaniment of Disestablishment. The more sectarian the

Church of England allows itself to become under the influence of the Anglo-Catholic section, the more unjust would appear the transfer of so great a national inheritance to its unregulated control. While in theory I am entirely in favour of Disestablishment and a large measure of Disendowment, my Nonconformist conscience, sensitive as it is, does not in practice command me to speak for such a far-reaching change for to me convincing reasons. It would not be in the interests of religion in its present perils from agnosticism and secularism to divide its forces as they would be by any such agitation. The growing fellowship and co-operation of the churches makes it inexpedient to introduce controversy and conflict. The invitation of the Lambeth Conference 1920 to all Christian people to recognise that God to-day by the signs of the times is showing His will to be the unity of the body of Christ, and the results of the conversations so far held between Anglicans and Nonconformists, hold out the hope that some day the solution of the problem will be found in a United Church independent of the State. Meanwhile this acquiescence does not involve the betrayal of the principle which it seems to me the Christian conscience must firmly maintain, that while God's authority as supreme extends over the State as well as the Church, the authority of the State, not absolute but only relative to its functions in Society, and as such to be respected and obeyed, cannot be recognised in the Church itself in its *soteriological* aspect as the *object* and the *organ* of the saving sovereignty of God in Christ, although in its *sociological* as a human society the State has the rights which its functions demand. Hence conscience may sometimes need to reject and resist law.

IN the preceding pages the nation has been assumed as the community, of which the State is the organ. The conviction has also been expressed that while we need not indulge in the theological abstraction that each nation is predetermined by divine creative decree, but may be regarded as a product of history, in which with the Hebrew prophets we may trace the Divine Providence; yet so far as we can foresee, the differences of nations will continue, and within the growing unity of mankind there will remain political divisions. Christianity, however, is marked by its *universalism*; and this truth must affect our ultimate interpretation of the relation of Church and State; this universalism as applied to the Church we may call *œcumenicity*, and to the State *internationalism*; and it is these three related conceptions which this last chapter will explore.

(1) Christian *universalism* has its roots in the Christian conception of God. As there is one God and Father of all, one Lord and Saviour of

all, and one Spirit in all, so there is only one human race, the object of the redemption from sin and the reconciliation to God which the Christian Gospel proclaims to all the world. The religion antecedent to Christianity, Judaism, was national, and as has already been mentioned, Church and State were one. But in the remnant of Isaiah a separation already begins. In Jeremiah and Ezekiel individualism in the relation of God and man emerges, when the nation as a unity ceased to be. But individualism leads on to *universalism*, of which there is a beginning in Isaiah xix. 19–25. The book of Jonah, which does not belong to the prophetic literature, but is the story about a prophet, tells how the missionary function of Israel was first refused and then accepted; and the vision of Isaiah liii. is of a nation which as martyr is missionary. While Jesus necessarily confined His ministry to " the lost sheep of the house of Israel," for His mission was primarily as Messiah to the chosen people, yet His message of the Heavenly Father, and His attitude to the outcasts of the Jewish society, to the Samaritans and the Gentiles, show that His heart was not bounded by Jewish particularism. Patriot he was, but not nationalist; Paul did not misunderstand the mind of Christ or act contrary to His intentions when he carried the Gospel to the Gentiles,

o

and explicitly declared this universalism. " I am debtor both to Greeks and to Barbarians, both to the wise and to the foolish. So, as much as in me is, I am ready to preach the gospel to you also that are in Rome. For I am not ashamed of the gospel; for it is the power of God unto salvation to every one that believeth: to the Jew first and also to the Greek " (Rom. i. 14–16). " There can be neither Jew nor Greek, there can be neither bond nor free, there can be no male and female; for ye are all one man in Christ Jesus " (Gal. iii. 28). " Where there cannot be Greek and Jew, circumcision and uncircumcision, barbarian, Scythian, bondman, freeman; but Christ is all and in all " (Col. iii. 11). These declarations need further elucidation, so as to make clear all that they mean and involve.

(a) Paul does not affirm that all these differences must be abolished, but that the divisions which result from them must be transcended, and in some of the cases transcendence involves abolition. While in *Philemon* the apostle may appear to ignore his own principle that in Christ there is neither bond nor free, neither bondman nor freeman, as he sends the slave back to his master, and does not challenge the rights of the one or the duties of the other in that relation, yet the treatment as brother for

which he pleads carries implicitly the condemnation and the abolition of slavery as
inconsistent with Christian brotherhood.   Circumcision continued for Jewish converts, only
for Gentiles was it abolished; but in due course it
ceased to be practised in the Christian Church.
In some of his instructions about the place of
women in home and Church, the Apostle seems
to relapse to the Jewish standpoint; but this is
an inconsistency which in advanced Christian
communities is disappearing.   In the Christian
home the division of sex is transcended, " sublimated " in the mutual love, fidelity and devotion
of husband and wife.   Although it is impossible
to forecast the future, yet, as far as one can
now see, the differences of nations will continue,
but their divisions, and all the evils that result
therefrom, will be transcended, " sublimated "
in an internationalism, if only they will receive
and respond to " the ministry of reconciliation,"
which is entrusted to the Church.

(b) The necessary implication of this universalism in Christ cannot be evaded by that dualism,
which has already been referred to as the
limitation of Lutheranism.   It is illegitimate to
separate a man's life in Christ from his life in the
society to which he belongs.   Christ's authority
and influence are not only extensively, but also
intensively universal.   He is the Saviour and

Lord not only of all mankind, but also of the whole manhood of each man. It is a Christian's duty not only to be a Christian in society, of necessity compromising with what is unchristian in it; it is his duty to do all that he can so to Christianise that society that he will be able to live fully as a Christian in all his relations. This comprehensive view of the Christian life has, however, been so expounded and emphasised in this volume, that attention to it need only be called here. What holds of the relation of men to one another holds of the relations of nations with such modifications in the application as the distinctive functions of the State demand; but the application must always be the maximum practicable and not the minimum, which even Christian men are in a false nationalism prepared to tolerate. This application will be more fully described when we come to the discussion of internationalism.

(c) It is necessary for a Christian to be a realist as well as an idealist; he must take account of facts; and there are many facts to confirm this universalism and not only to allow, but even to ask for its application. Anthropology justifies the assumption of a common origin for the whole human race, a natural unity of all mankind. Even the most obvious difference of colour is explicable biologically without assuming a

separate origin. The assertion of a difference of
mentality between the civilised and uncivilised
peoples finds no justification in comparative
psychology, as some of the traits of the savage
survive in the illiterate in a civilised community
and even appear in the child at a certain stage
of development. Despite all that learning,
vitiated by prejudice, may assert, there is no
ground for exalting one people to permanent
superiority, and humiliating another to permanent
inferiority. There is a common human nature;
within it there are good stocks and bad, but
these do not correspond to colour or nation;
nurture in the widest sense largely accounts for
differences, " All men have sinned and come
short of the glory of God " (Rom. iii. 23), and
God in Christ is reconciling the world unto
Himself (II Cor. v. 19). Still more importance
attaches to the growing unification of the world.
Geographical exploration has opened up all the
lands; the means of transport—railway, steam-
ship, aeroplane—and communication—telegraph,
telephone, wireless—are lessening the handicap
to intercourse from distances in space and dura-
tion in time. Conquest, colonisation, commerce,
industry and science are promoting a common
civilisation and culture. It is the moral and
religious unification which lags behind, and yet
without this a common standard of morals to

regulate conduct, and a common faith as the sustaining motive of that standard this unification may bring, nay, is bringing, discord and conflict; neighbours are not always neighbourly, and these contacts may provoke irritation and friction, unless the spirit of conciliation and community is infused into all relations. Hence this Christian universalism, confirmed as it is by the facts of nature and of history, must not be allowed to remain an ideal and aspiration; it must be translated into word and deed. If mankind is one in Christ, then all men should be won for Christ. A universal religion like the Christian must be missionary in effort, and must realise that only as missionary can it be true to itself.

(d) The significance of the foreign mission enterprise is not fully recognised by many of its supporters, still less by those who are indifferent to it. So long as its sole object is conceived to be individual conversions and the formation of separate churches, it will not command the attention that it deserves. What is involved, rightly apprehended, is the unification of the world not only in one civilisation and one culture, but also in common moral standards and religious convictions, moralising and spiritualising that civilisation and culture. In the international relations how essential is it that there should be a recognition of mutual obligations from the standpoint of Christian ethics! In politics how urgent that the value of the individual man and social solidarity should be recognised as in the Christian conception of human brotherhood based on divine Fatherhood! Even in economics how important that the standard of living among the tribes now barbarous should be raised, and thus the peril to white labour from cheaper coloured labour should be averted! Christendom has not solved its own problems; but it could and would did nominally Christian peoples become actually Christian, practising what they profess. When we think of what Europe and America can do for world prosperity, security, peace and progress, we are too prone to forget to take account of Africa and Asia. Nevertheless, a perilous factor in the world's history even now are Japan, China, India; and in the future Africa also will come upon the stage for the world-drama. The motive of Christian missions has been above all the constraining love of Christ, and it ought to continue to be so; but this motive would not be weakened were all that Christ can mean for the human race as universal Saviour and Lord realised. There is no contemporary reference to the ministry of Jesus, outside of the Gospels, and yet that ministry is slowly and surely transforming the world; so " the wisdom of this world " is not giving any heed, or at best only scant heed, to the work of evangelising the world; and yet, if man's relation to God is the supreme concern, that enterprise has more promise and potency for the world's progress than the policies and diplomacies of the Great Powers, even than the League of Nations.

(e) It is evident that the problem of the relation of Church and State is of growing importance in the foreign field, and presents peculiar problems, as difficult of solution as any which now occupy Christendom. Owing to the influence of the nations, from which the missionaries come, there is generally toleration; but with the growing sense of independent nationality, should paganism gain control of the governments, that toleration may cease. In Japan the reverence for the Emperor which is required as a sign of loyalty, a pledge of patriotism, is raising a difficulty for Christians, similar to that in the Roman Empire. In China religious instruction is more subject to control than it was, and the law, if strictly enforced, might offer an obstacle to the use of education in evangelism. Much as one may desire self-determination for India, how Christian missions will fare in the new India is a question which may be asked with some anxiety. Yet these very difficulties come as a challenge to the Christian Church to continue, and even increase, its efforts to give to the world that life with God in Christ, in which alone mankind can fulfil its divinely-appointed destiny. It is, however, not merely the tolerance now enjoyed that is to be desired.   It is the transformation of pagan into Christian societies with Christian standards and institutions which is to be the aim; and thus abroad, as at home, that wider view of Christianity as the leaven transforming all the meal of human thought and life must be recognised in all missionary methods. Should the totalitarian State, still pagan, emerge on the mission field, the totalitarian Church must be prepared to meet its challenge.   Conflicts now witnessed in Europe may in future have their stage in Asia and Africa.   Probably more than for many centuries the Church will need to be the Church militant, yet confident that in the end it will be the Church triumphant.

(*f*) My interest in the subject must be my excuse for adding a paragraph on the strategy of missions in this conflict.   There appeared in 1933 under the title *Rethinking Missions* the Report of an American Commission, almost entirely lay, which visited India, Ceylon, Burma, China and Japan to survey the work of American Missions in order to assure the supporters that they were not wasting their wealth on an object not worth while.   The practical American mind must be sure that it is making sound investments with its money. The verdict is favourable, but a number of criticisms are offered, and comments made which deserve notice, although it must here be very summary. While the Commissioners place a Christian theism and a Christian altruism alongside of personal loyalty to Christ as a motive, I think it can be confidently said that it is this personal loyalty which is the prevailing motive among missionaries, and that a Christian theism or Christian altruism would not be adequate without it and is indeed dependent upon it. The Commissioners rightly urge that the missionary's attitude to the religions he encounters be not only tolerant, but also sympathetic and appreciative, looking for the points of contact and the lines of least resistance, recognising the best, and using that as a stepping-stone to Christ. An increasing number of missionaries take that attitude, and most of them are being trained to do it. But when the Commissioners argue that the missionary must be learner as well as teacher, that the sharing must be mutual, a question must be pressed. That the missionary himself may learn in contact with other religions, to apprehend his own Christian faith more adequately, and to discount national and sectarian accretions which do not belong to its substance may be fully conceded. But that the Gospel is not a complete message from God to man, and needs to be supplemented from other religions, that Christ needs Confucius, Gautama, or Mohammed as His complement may I, with all respect, yet very confidently, deny, and I speak as one who for thirty years taught the history and the philosophy of religion. This depreciation of the uniqueness of Christ, man's necessity for Him, and His sufficiency for man, explains their insistence that the benefits of Christianity in education and healing should be imparted for their own sakes as Christian service without any evangelism. Great as are these gifts of Christian philanthropy and fully as they should be rendered, it is Christ Himself who is the supreme value; and it is a wrong to give the good without seeking to share the best. Evangelism should be unobtrusive, considerate, patient; grace should be offered graciously; but all men need Him, and He seeks all men. Lastly the message suggested by the Commission is less sufficient for human need than the Gospel which to all men is " the power and the wisdom of God unto salvation."

(2) Whether the Church as it now exists is fit and worthy to be the herald of so universal a revelation of God and redemption of man may be doubted. If instead of one Church, the

community of the Spirit, the body of Christ, the world sees a number of churches, not recognising one another's ministries, not sharing the same sacraments, not making one confession of faith, not working together in love, not sustained by one hope, it is a cruel jest, a vain mockery to say that there is a spiritual unity, and that that unity is not inconsistent with, although it may not be manifest, in the variety of interpretations and organisations. In God's Universe the invisible becomes visible, the form is actualised in matter, the soul expresses itself in look, gesture, speech. God's providence is disclosed in the events of history, " the Word became flesh," the one Spirit of God must also be audible and tangible in the one body of Christ. To realise the divine purpose in history, to make effective the divine truth and grace in the world, to be the totalitarian Church, the obstacle of division must be removed, and the unity must be recognised by the world. Unity does not mean uniformity; not difference or variety is the hindrance, but division. In the movements towards the recovery of unity the word œcumenicity has on the Continent come into general use; in Sweden, for instance, an advocate of such unity is called an " œcumen," most notable of all was the late Archbishop of Uppsala, Dr. Nathan Söderblom. It is convenient to use this term in the ecclesiastical sphere, and to confine the word international to the political.

(a) In insisting on œcumenicity, the recognition of the oneness of all the Christian churches in Christ as a reason for reunion, one pronounces no uncharitable judgment on the past, one does not lower one's appreciation for the fidelity, courage and sacrifice of men who followed the lead of conscience as they apprehended it at any cost, one recognises that the division was more often due to an intolerant majority than to a recalcitrant minority, and that division was not in motive and intention the sin of schism. There were historical causes of divisions, which forbid an adverse judgment on those responsible for them. Nevertheless to-day there is the growing conviction that the Spirit of God is saying to the churches, " Make manifest your unity in Christ." The defence which is offered for the divisions of the Christian Church, not only in the past, but in the present, is that each of the denominations emphasises, brings into prominence, some aspect of Christian truth and life which otherwise would be neglected or forgotten, e.g. Congregationalism stands for the liberty of the laity; Presbyterianism for the equality of the ministry; Episcopacy for the authority which order in belief and worship demands. I use these illustrations without committing myself to the adequacy of any of these claims. But to this plea a threefold answer can be given.

Firstly, we cannot treat the Church of Christ as if one member of the body could be severed from the others, and retain its due proportion and subordination. What a monstrosity a body would be if one limb were swelled out and the others shrunken! I am reminded of the cartoons in a Glasgow comic paper, in which to a huge head was attached a small body. Must it not be confessed that the divisions of Christendom do thus misrepresent what the Church should be in the due proportion and subordination of the parts to the whole? Is it not time for the Church to try to recover the symmetry which will present to the world its wholeness in thought and life?

Secondly, this emphasis on one or other aspect of the whole, instead of the whole, produces in individuals a narrowness and pettiness of outlook which makes it impossible for them to draw waters of refreshment from anything but their own village pump. Some authentic illustrations may be offered. An old Presbyterian lady was taken by some friends to a Baptist church to see the rite of immersion. The preacher so set forth the necessity of this form, that when she was asked what she thought of the sermon, she expressed herself in her Aberdonian speech thus: " Yon wee mannie thinks ower muckle o' his wee tubbie." An Edinburgh minister was preaching in a Highland church, and gave out a paraphrase. After the precentor had twice remonstrated: "We dinna sing paraphrases here," he gave out the metrical psalm which begins with the words: "Lord bless and pity us." A missionary for many years in Central Africa was refused the communion by an Anglican curate, because he had not been confirmed; and the missionary properly replied: "Keep your own table; it is not the Lord's." These cases prove how great is the danger in laying stress on minor details instead of thinking and living in the largeness and wholeness of the one Church of Christ. May we not hope for the time when the emphasis of the Baptist and the Anglican will seem as mistaken as that of the Presbyterian?

Lastly, in any scheme of reunion there should be no excluded elements of the Christian belief, worship or polity. There are personal preferences, for now we know only in part (I Cor. xiii. 12), and there should be room in the unity of the Church for all the variety which is consistent with harmony, effective concord and co-operation.

(*b*) However necessary reunion may appear, the omens are not altogether favourable. At the Lausanne Conference of 1927 many were as concerned about asserting differences as about

recognising agreements; and there are still some
of the Churches who are hesitant about what
seems the inevitable next step, the closer scrutiny
of the agreements to find in them the reason for
and the motive of reconciling the differences.
The proposed Conference of 1937 will more fully
deserve the censure too hastily passed on the
Conference of 1927 of being a fiasco and futility
if it does not mark some progress in that direction,
not necessarily a solution of the problems, but
at least a greater willingness to consider their
possibility. Some of the Replies to the Reports
show a satisfaction and complacency with these
differences which are disappointing, as a selection
of these in the volume *Convictions* proves.

(i) The immediate situation—the peril to the
independence of the Churches from the totalitarian state—should strengthen the aspiration
after unity. It is being shown that in division
there is weakness. Recognising that in the
Roman Catholic Church it was dealing with a
world-wide Church, strong in its unity, the Nazi
Government of Germany did not delay to come
to an understanding with Rome. Attempts to
violate the conditions of the Concordat are
being made, and there is unauthorised talk about
one German Church; but the Hitler régime will
show itself more reckless than it has as yet been,
if it presses its challenge of the authority of the

Papacy. A divided Protestantism seemed easier to handle, but some competent observers hold that it would have had less recognition of its independence and been treated more drastically had not the Roman Catholic Church already secured its Concordat. Had Protestantism represented a universal Church, and not territorial churches within a merely national federation, one may venture to believe there would have been more hesitation. The Protestant Churches outside of Germany shrank from intervening at the beginning, as their *locus standi* in a domestic German dispute might have been questioned, and the opposition in Germany at first deprecated any intervention. It was the Universal Council of Life and Work which felt entitled to take public action on the occasion of the claim of the official organisation of the National Church to be alone representative of the Churches in Germany. But voluntary and temporary support cannot have the same effectiveness as would the constant general influence of a Protestantism adequately a manifest unity.

(ii) The situation in Germany illustrates one of the dangers of the divisions of Christendom. Corrupt and superstitious, intolerant and tyrannical as was the Mediæval Church—and much sentimental nonsense is talked and written about its merits—it did assert the supra-national

P

character of the Church of Christ, its transcendence of the authority of the State. Great as were the moral and religious gains, although they were not all as unmixed boons as an ignorant and fanatical Protestantism represents them as being, one evil the Reformation brought with it—the nationalisation of the Churches. One of the political factors of that change was the desire and effort for national independence, which saw in the authority of Rome a galling foreign yoke; but in all Protestant countries at the time the prince took the place of the Pope, and the State assumed control of the Church. The mentality of the German State to-day was the mentality of the English and the Scottish States in the sixteenth and the seventeenth centuries. And this close connection with the State carried the further consequence that the national type of thought and life came to dominate the Church to a degree inconsistent with its universalism. As the environment does and must exercise an influence on the organism, and it must adapt itself, or modify its environment if it can, in order to survive, so the Christian Church cannot escape the influence of its historical situation: if it has wings to soar into the heavens, it must also have feet planted on the earth. We must admit that the Christian Church of the early centuries could not altogether escape the influence of Roman imperialism in its polity, and of Greek intellectualism in its theology, yet the accommodation went so far as to imperil distinctively Christian characteristics. A nationalised Church has succumbed to a narrower environment, and runs more risk of being provincial: and it can preserve itself only by œcumenicity.   Lutheranism in Germany is a more nationalised type of religion than is represented by even the Reformed Churches of Germany, for they look back to Geneva, not Wittenberg, and they have kept their contacts with the Reformed Churches of Switzerland, Hungary, Czecho-Slovakia, Holland and Great Britain.   Although Anglicanism is represented wherever English-speaking people go, it is, as the name indicates, distinctively English in its merits as in its defects.   Scottish Presbyterianism has also its local limitations, and I am sorry, much as I desired the union of the Presbyterian Churches, that the united Church attaches so much importance to the description of itself as *national*.   It has cherished the œcumenic spirit in doing as much as it has done for the Reformed Churches of the Continent, and its Universities have shown that same œcumenicity in the bestowal of its honorary doctorate in divinity. While the influence of environment cannot be altogether escaped, it should always be subordinated to Christian universalism, and the Church must be free in Christ from all dependence on the State. In a previous chapter I have tried to discuss the question how far the conscience of a Free Churchman, as I am mind and soul, can be tolerant to the existence of an Established Church. In all the conversations at Lambeth with the Church of England it has been made clear that the Free Churches will never return to " the house of bondage " of an Establishment.

(iii) The goal of reunion may still be far off, but the course towards it is at our feet. Each Christian Church will realise its own character as Christian in the measure in which it ceases to be sectarian, in which it assigns to its differences from other Churches a growingly subordinate place to its agreements, as it abides in " the unity of the Spirit in the bond of peace," as it recognises its obligations to, and responsibilities for, the good of other Churches so far as it has the ability and the opportunity to share with them what God has given to it. While interference there cannot be, yet surely there may be, not encouragement only, but remonstrance also. While the official spokesmen of the National Church in Germany protest their œcumenicity, their desire to maintain intimate relations with other Churches, they express their resentment at any adverse judgment on their policy, and thus betray their failure to understand that the relations of Churches in Christ must transcend national frontiers; that in the Church of Christ there are no foreigners or aliens, but that all are natives as born of the one Spirit. It is only in its œcumenicity, transcending all national limitations, that the Church can dare to speak to the national states in the name of the one God who is above all, and can claim an authority in that Name which no State can rival.

(3) The universalism of Christianity cannot be confined to the relation of the Churches: it must be extended to the relation of the nations to one another. This seemingly obvious inference has, however, been recently challenged by an apologist for the " German Christian " policy. He asserts that œcumenicity has nothing to do with internationalism or pacifism; but in this declaration he offers a proof of how Christianity has been nationalised in this party, and has lost much that is distinctive of it.

(a) When discussing the functions of the State, it was assumed that the State with which we are at present concerned is the organ of community for the nation. As far as one can infer from the history of the past what the developments of the future will be, it is not likely that nations will cease to exist as independent associations, whatever limitations they may accept on their absolute sovereignty from the League of Nations. We do not yet see " the Parliament of men, the Federation of the world." While the Church should use all the influence it can command to scrap such limitations as the common good of mankind may require, it is not, in my judgment, under any obligation to depreciate nationality or to desire the extinction of national independence. It is not *cosmopolitanism*, which claims to be superior to the sentiment of nationality, which is the Church's necessary ideal, but *internationalism*, which recognises the differences of the nations, but subordinates them to the unity of mankind.

(*b*) Much confusion is caused by the ambiguity of words. Owing to recent excesses *nationalism* is a term which has come into disrepute, and it might be preferable, if it were possible, to confine it to the abuse of a legitimate and commendable sentiment, and to use the word *patriotism*, for the love of the fatherland and mother-speech, which is entirely consistent with the Christian love of mankind. Just as a father has a primary, but not exclusive obligation to his own family, so a nation has to its own citizens, their security, prosperity and progress; and in this sense nationalism is not to be condemned. Only when self-interest is pursued regardless of injury to others, is nationalism an evil. It is only as each nation bears its own burden of responsibility, that the nations can bear one another's burdens (Gal. vi. 2, 5). Lest there be misunderstanding, let me add that it is not only in foreign, but also in domestic policy that a nation must consider whether in pursuing its own interests it is inflicting injury on others.

(c) In my judgment a great deal, if not all, *economic nationalism*, as it is now being practised, is from the Christian standpoint wrong. The restriction on foreign imports, which other lands can produce more cheaply than our country itself can, is not only lowering our invisible exports, shipping, banking, insurance, and so making us less capable of paying for what we must import, but it is inflicting hardship and loss on countries which depended for their prosperity on our markets, and which consequently cannot afford to pay for the exports which we desire to send them to meet their wants, nor the interest on the investments of capital from this country for their economic development. There is what might be called economic nationalism which cannot be so condemned. A nation should develop its own national resources and employ its own people as fully as it can with economic advantage, the production of as much wealth to meet its people's wants as possible; it should so distribute that wealth throughout the community, that the standard of living being generally raised, there will be wider markets at home for the goods it produces; and there will need to be less dependence on foreign markets in its exports and less dangerous competition with other industrialised nations. For it must be admitted that the Christian ideal of free trade, the closest possible relations of nations to one another in the mutual supply of their needs, has not proved impracticable, but it has not been practised. As long as commerce is regarded as conflict, and the mentality of war is applied in it, as long as imports from another land are regarded as an injury inflicted by it, and yet exports are regarded as a benefit to it, the Golden Rule of doing unto others as we desire to be done unto is being disregarded, and the consequence of international trade which should unite the nations is prejudice, suspicion, hostility. Each nation wants to sell as much to other nations, and buy as little from them as possible, forgetting that nations can buy only as they sell, that commerce should be co-operation and not conflict. As now conducted, international trade is a danger more than a boon; and, unless there is a change, wars in the future are more likely to arise from economic causes rather than from any others. As an immediate policy it would seem prudent for many nations to try to extend their home rather than their foreign markets.

(d) There is this paradox that international trade is now a threat rather than an encouragement to Christian internationalism, because here, as in the economic system generally, self-interest has become too dominant a motive and competition too prevalent a method. Hence Christian internationalists show only their ignorance and incompetence if they think they can prevent war and promote peace by a sentimental cultivation of friendship, while disregarding the defects in the economic system which are thus vitiating international trade, poisoning the very currents of international relations which should be for the refreshing of the life of the peoples. I have tried in a previous book, *Can Christ Save Society?* to expose these defects. Reference to this subject, however, was here inevitable, as the Christian Temple of Peace can be built surely only on the foundations of economic righteousness. Hence the objects of the *World Alliance for International Friendship through the Churches*, and that of *The Universal Council of Christian Life and Work* are complementary. All interests, activities and relations within each nation must be cleansed and hallowed by the Spirit of Christ, if *internationalism* in the broad sense of all international relations is to be not a peril but a promise of better days for the world, if recovery and not ruin is to be the issue of the world crisis.

(*e*) This Christian internationalism will not command the authority among the nations it needs, as long as the world hears only the confused voices of a multitude of Churches, instead of the voice of the one Church. For that one voice we need not wait till all ecclesiastical organisations are brought together; but all Christians whom the spirit of œcumenicity unites can bear a common testimony and wield a common influence. That Christian internationalism also may be derided, if the world as a whole remains unevangelised, and paganism in many forms becomes the rival of the Christian faith. The foreign mission enterprise which seeks to win the world for Christ must be advanced, if the Kingdoms of the world are to become the Kingdom of our God and of His Christ.

(4) In closing, a few sentences may be added to justify the title of this volume, which for me at least is no arbitrary choice, but arises out of the contents and the convictions which lie behind it.

(*a*) The associations of the word *sovereignty* in Christian theology have often been repellent. God has been represented as an Eastern Despot, doing as He pleases, and not always pleasing good for man, and therefore I have avoided it in the title, although, when the theological standpoint was made clear in the first chapter, I have not hesitated about its use. I have not used the word *Kingdom*, because of the common misunderstanding of the phrase *the Kingdom of God*, as a human society subject to God's will, with a false emphasis on what man ought to do, instead of on what God has done, is doing, and will do; it is not the *realm* among men, but the *rule* of God which must be primary and directive in our thinking. With Calvinism and with Barthianism I affirm the sovereignty of God, and man's dependence on God for every good. Not as a human society, its *sociological* aspect, can the Church confidently confront the State when it claims absolute authority in the *total* life of man. Only in its *soteriological* aspect as the object and the organ of God's supreme saving activity can it command the divine resources of truth and grace which alone can overcome, as alone able to save the world.

(*b*) To bring out the distinctive character of God's sovereignty in the Christian revelation and redemption, I have used the term *fatherly* as God's Fatherhood revealed in Christ, and realised in us by the Spirit is the distinctive Christian conception of God. In the combination *fatherly rule*, the adjective is protected against the weak sentimentalism which regards God's love as good nature, indifferent to sin, and the noun against the harsh dogmatism which has for so long and so often hidden the Heavenly Father's face from His earthly children. Throughout this volume I have tried to keep the balance even of God's judgment and mercy. If in the State men must still experience God's rule as *law*, through the Church they should learn that it is meant to be a servant of *grace*.

" Thine is Judæ's law, with love beside,
    The truth that censures, and the grace that saves."

NOTE TO CHAPTER V

As it would have interrupted the continuity of the treatment, I have reserved for this Note the inclusion of some interesting documents which throw fuller light on the situation:

(1) In June those opposed to the German Christian policy of the assimilation of Church and State met at Barmen, and constituted themselves as the " Confessional Synod " as " a church opposition on the basis of six evangelical principles."

" 1. Jesus Christ, as He is revealed to us in the Holy Gospel, is the only word of God, which we hear, which we have to trust and obey in life and in death. The heresy is refuted that the Church can and must recognise, in addition to this one word, other events and powers, figures, and truths as the revelation of God.

2. God, through Jesus Christ, claims our whole life. The heresy is refuted that there can be spheres of life in which we do not belong to Him, but to other masters.

3. The Christian Church is a community of brethren and belongs solely to Christ. The heresy is refuted that the Church can do with its mission and its organisation as it likes and surrender it to the vagaries of temporarily prevailing philosophical and political convictions.

4. The offices of the Church are not there to give one man dominion over another, but for the exercise of the administration entrusted to and required of the whole community. The heresy is refuted that the Church can and should, apart from this ministration, give itself, or allow itself to be given, leaders endowed with ruling powers.

5. The Gospel tells us that the State has the divine task of looking after law and order in a world not yet delivered, a world in which the Church also stands. The Church recognises in gratitude and reverence to God the benefits of this His commandment. The heresy is refuted that the State, over and above its special task, should and can become the single and total regulator of human life and thus also fulfil the vocation of the Church. The heresy is also refuted that the Church, above and beyond its own special task, should assume State characteristics, State tasks, and State dignities and thereby itself become an organ of the State.

6. The mission of the Church, in which its freedom is rooted, consists in the preaching to all people, in Christ's stead and therefore in the service of His Word, the message of the mercy of God. The heresy is refuted that the Church can place the word and works of the Lord at the service of any arbitrarily chosen wishes, aims and plans."

(2) The gage of battle was still more definitely thrown down in a Declaration, which challenged the legitimate authority of the Synod which had supported and approved the policy of the Reichs Bishop, and summoned the Churches to disobey.

The Declaration Read at the Meeting of Sunday, August 12th, at the Gemarkenkirche, Barmen, before 1800 members of the Barmen Confessional Synod representing the Opposition to the present Church Government of Mueller.

" On August 9th a meeting constituted in a manner which is essentially unconstitutional made decisions, enacted laws, and declared right and constitutional wrongs which have been practised hitherto by the Reich Church Government.

This so-called National Synod and its decisions and deliberations are all invalid according to principles of ecclesiastical and civil law.

Whosoever complies is (therefore) himself guilty of breaking the Constitution and violating the laws of the Church. We refuse so to do and call upon the Congregations and Churches that on their part they should not become guilty of compliance with these breaches of the Constitution and of right.

That things should come to such a pass is due to the continuous unecclesiastical conduct of the National Church Government, especially to the conduct of the Reichs Bishop, who was called to protect the Constitution of the German Evangelical Church.

The Reich Church Government despises the simple fundamentals of law and justice. It submits the preaching of the Gospel to force and might of fallible men.

It is devoid of that brotherly love made obligatory by the Holy Scriptures. Thereby it forsakes the fundamentals of the Reformation Churches built upon the Gospel.

He who consciously breaks laws and constitutional principles which it is his personal duty to defend has by his own acts foregone the right to expect obedience.

He who, though called to the leadership of the Churches, incessantly forsakes both Christian teaching and the Christian Gospel, puts himself outside the Church.

Therefore we declare to the Churches, the people of the congregations, and their fellow members, as we stand responsible to God:

Obedience to this Church Government is Disobedience to God!

Nevertheless the foundation of God standeth sure having this seal: The Lord knoweth them that are His, and let every one that nameth the name of Christ depart from iniquity." (2 Timothy ii. 19.)

(*Signed*) THE FRATERNAL COUNCIL
(*Der Bruderrat*)

(3) It need hardly be said that the sympathy of the
Christian Churches outside of Germany has been with the
opposition, but public action was not at once taken lest it
might throw open the opposition to the taunt that support
was being sought abroad in a domestic controversy con-
cerning Germany only; but, as the National Church claimed
representation on the Universal Christian Council of Life
and Work, sent delegates, and insisted on the exclusion of
the representatives of the Opposition, action became inevitable, and the following resolution was adopted :—

" 1. The Universal Christian Council for Life and Work,
meeting at Fanoe, August 24th–30th, 1934, after common
prayer and consideration of problems which at the present
day confront the Church throughout the entire world, has
resolved to invite the Christian Churches to undertake
during the next few years in international co-operation and
œcumenical fellowship a fresh examination of the problems
of the relations between the Church, the State, and the
Community in the light of the fundamental conceptions of
the Christian faith.

2. Grave anxiety was expressed by the representatives of
the Churches in many different countries lest vital principles
of Christian liberty should be endangered or compromised
at the present time in the life of the German Evangelical
Church. The Universal Christian Council believes that it
is the special task of the œcumenical movement to express
and deepen the sense of mutual responsibility in all parts of
the Christian Church. And accordingly,

> Animated by feelings of cordial goodwill to the
> German people,
> Profoundly grateful for the invaluable contribution
> of the German Evangelical Church to the life and
> theological thought of Christendom,
> Dissociating itself from every political motive,

Recognising the peculiar difficulties of a situation of revolution, and

Acknowledging the sins and shortcomings of the Churches which its members severally represent,

The Council declares its conviction that autocratic Church rule, especially when imposed upon the conscience in solemn oath; the use of methods of force; and the suppression of free discussion are incompatible with the true nature of the Christian Church, and asks in the name of the Gospel for its fellow-Christians in the German Evangelical Church

freedom to preach the Gospel of our Lord Jesus Christ and to live according to His teaching,

freedom of the printed word and of assembly in the service of the Christian Community,

freedom for the Church to instruct its youth in the principles of Christianity, and immunity from the compulsory imposition of a philosophy of life antagonistic to the Christian religion.

3. The Council approves and endorses the steps taken in its name by its President, the Bishop of Chichester.

4. The Council desires to convey its sympathy to all its fellow Christians in Germany in the difficulties and perplexities of the present time, and to remain in friendly contact with all groups in the German Evangelical Church.

5. The Council desires to assure its brethren in the Confessional Synod of the German Evangelical Church of its prayers and heartfelt sympathy in their witness to the principles of the Gospel, and of its resolve to maintain close fellowship with them.

6. The Council instructs the Administrative Committee to take whatever steps are judged most appropriate and

Q

desirable to communicate the concern expressed in this resolution to the authorities and members of the German Evangelical Church, and to follow up the principles which it sets out."

(4) The German Delegation protested in the following terms:

" The German Delegation expresses its gratitude for the brotherly spirit shown to a large extent during the session of the Universal Christian Council this year at Fanoe. The Delegation further expresses its thanks that a real effort has been made in the above resolution to speak with under-standing and a full sense of responsibility, and even in this time of conflict to consolidate the bonds between the German Church and the Œcumenical Movement. In spite of this, the German Delegation finds itself unable to give its vote to the above resolution. The Delegation repeats the opinion which it has frequently expressed that public resolutions cannot help the inner developments in the Church in Germany. It is our conviction that the Univer-sal Christian Council must keep clearly before its eyes and consider with a special sense of responsibility the limits of its œcumenical task in relation to the inner affairs of one of its member Churches. It must do this for the sake of the future of the Œcumenical Movement itself. The German Delegation believes that the new epoch in the life of the German people and in the life of the German Church has thrown up a rich variety of positive problems for the Churches of the World. And it is also confident that the Church of the German Reformation, according to God's gracious will, will itself master its present difficulties. The German Delegation believes that it is not for us as Christians to ask for the help of men, but to appeal in the spirit of deepest seriousness to the saving help and power of God. In particular the German Delegation protests, for the reasons which have been given in detail to the Council, against the following points:

1. It rejects the interpretation that there is in the German Church ' autocratic rule.' What is described as ' autocratic Church rule ' is in fact the concentration of the Church administration and measures of ecclesiastical procedure.

2. The German Delegation repudiates the view that in the German Reich the free preaching of the Gospel, in written and spoken word, is in any way endangered or that due protection is not afforded to the Christian education of Youth. It attests, on the contrary, that the general situation in the Germany of to-day gives far more possibility for the preaching of the Gospel than ever before.

3. The German Delegation rejects the one-sided stress on a particular group in the German Church and the approval given by the Council to the special theological view of that group. The Delegation finds in this an attitude to the internal situation of the German Church which transgresses the limits of the task of the Universal Christian Council in a very questionable way."

Despite this Protest the Council has invited representation of the Confessional Synod. While great indignation at its action has been expressed by the official organisation in Germany, membership in the Council has not been withdrawn. There is ground for the belief that the German Government itself is sensitive regarding the opinion of the Churches abroad, especially in Great Britain and America. These documents have been reproduced with the permission of the Secretary, from one of the pamphlets, *The Church–State Struggle in Germany*, by Rev. H. S. Leiper, issued by The Friends of Europe.

SOME USEFUL BOOKS AND PAMPHLETS

1. *Religion and the European Mind*, by Adolf Keller.
2. *Recent Developments in German Protestantism*, by Otto Piper.
3. *The Church Controversy in Germany*, by Anders Nygren.
4 and 5. *Die Œcumenische Aufgabe der deutschen evangelischen Kirche*, and *Die evangelische Kirche im neuen Reich*, by F. W. Krummacher. (Defence of the " German Christian " policy.)
6. *Das Volk und die Lehre der evangelischen Kirche*, by H. Sasse. (Standpoint of the " Confessional Church.")
7. *Mythos und Offenbarung*, by Karl Witte. (Exposure of the Neo-Paganism in Germany.)
8. *Die Anfänge der Religion by Arianer und Israeliten*, by Arthur Titius. (Exposure of the pretensions of the " German Faith " movement.)
9. *Kirche und Judenchristen*, by D. G. Kittel. (Proposal that Hebrew Christians should form a separate Church for their distinctive witness to the Messiah.)
10. " Friends of Europe " Publications include several pamphlets on the Church Controversy in Germany.

INDEX

1. *Names*

2. *Scripture References*